Family Circle | **soups and sandwiches cookbook**

Family Circle ®

SOUPS and SANDWICHES
COOKBOOK

FAMILY CIRCLE LIBRARY OF CREATIVE COOKING

**A Practical Guide to creative cooking containing special material from Family Circle
Magazine and the Family Circle Illustrated Library of Cooking**

ROCKVILLE HOUSE PUBLISHERS
GARDEN CITY, NEW YORK 11530

on the cover:
Boothbay Chowder is a Down-East favorite that will satisfy even hearty appetites.

on the back cover:
When it's too hot to cook, put together this colorful and nutritious combination—a meal-in-one super sandwich, **Provençal Pan Bagna,** and a hot or cold soup, **Tomato and Zucchini Soup.**

opposite title page:
There are heroes and there are heroes. This one with its mound of red and green peppers and cheese and anchovy fillets is the **Super Cheese Hero.**

Publishing Staff

Editor: MALCOLM E. ROBINSON
Design and Layout: MARGOT L. WOLF
Production Editor: DONALD D. WOLF

For Family Circle

Editorial Director: ARTHUR M. HETTICH
Editor Family Circle Books: MARIE T. WALSH
Assistant Editor: CERI E. HADDA

A QUICK METRIC TABLE FOR COOKS

Liquid Measures

1 liter	4¼ cups (1 quart + ¼ cup or 34 fluid ounces)	1 gallon	3.785 liters
1 demiliter (½ liter)	2⅛ cups (1 pint + ⅛ cups or 17 fluid ounces)	1 quart	0.946 liter
1 deciliter (1/10 liter)	A scant ½ cup or 3.4 fluid ounces	1 pint	0.473 liter
1 centiliter (1/100 liter)	Approximately 2 teaspoons or .34 fluid ounce	1 cup	0.237 liter or 237 milliliters
1 milliliter (1/1000 liter)	Approximately 1/5 teaspoon or .034 fluid ounce	1 tbsp.	Approximately 1.5 centiliters or 15 milliliters

Weights

1 kilogram	2.205 pounds	1 pound	0.454 kilogram or 453.6 grams
500 grams	1.103 pounds or about 17.5 ounces	½ pound	0.226 kilogram or 226.8 grams
100 grams	3.5 ounces	¼ pound	0.113 kilogram or 113.4 grams
10 grams	.35 ounce	1 ounce	28.35 grams
1 gram	0.035 ounce		

Linear Measures

1 meter	1.09 yards or 3.28 feet or 39.37 inches	1 yard	0.914 meter
1 decimeter (1/10 meter)	3.93 inches	1 foot	0.3048 meter or 3.048 decimeters or 30.48 centimeters
1 centimeter (1/100 meter)	0.39 inch	1 inch	2.54 centimeters or 25.4 millimeters
1 millimeter (1/1000 meter)	0.039 inch		

Contents

This smorgasbord of sandwiches includes (top to bottom): **Stuffed Ham Slices, Blue Cheese Open-Face Sandwich** with egg wedges, **Beef Rollups,** and two other blue cheese sandwiches with egg and apple garnishes (see index for individual recipes).

Introduction

BE GOOD TO YOURSELF. Don't spend time in the kitchen when you don't have to. When you'd much rather sit on the patio because it is hotter inside the house than outside, or when you are rushed and just want to relax with friends or family, turn to a quick soup and some nutritious sandwiches.

For one thing, most sandwiches are put together in a hurry, whether they are a meal-in-one hero complete with lashings of meats and cheeses and other accompaniments, an open-face sandwich brimming with left-over meat and simmering with a golden gravy, or just a peanut butter sandwich.

And they are the one meal that takes care of how hungry you are at the moment. Whether it is the mouth-filling hero or a dainty finger sandwich, you are sure to satisfy yourself and your guests.

But soups and sandwiches are more than just fast-meals or appetite pleasers; they can set the tone of an evening. For example, a bowl of hot vegetable soup and a hearty beef sandwich placed before an open-fire of a winter's evening is sure to please guests, and set the evening off on the right foot.

To take care of your needs and to make it easy for you to find what you want, your **Soups and Sandwiches Cookbook** is divided into two main chapters. The first one is for sandwiches, and here the chapter is divided so that you don't have to figure out what type of sandwich is where. If you want a dagwood, you'll find it in the section titled dagwoods.

The soup chapter is also divided. If you want a cheese soup, or one with vegetables, or just a clear soup, check in these sections.

Enjoy your **Soups and Sandwiches Cookbook** and let it give you the ease and the pleasure it was specifically designed to.

Sandwiches to Suit Every Occasion

Many times, a sandwich fits the bill. Whether meal-in-one heroes or hoboes, or dainty party sandwiches, and whether they are open or closed, large or small, plain or fancy, you'll find a wide assortment to choose from in these pages.

HEARTY HEROES AND HOBOES

California Biddy Bunwiches

A new version of chicken salad with tangy golden pineapple and crunchy almonds

Makes 6 servings

2 whole chicken breasts (about 1½ pounds)
2 cups water
1 medium-size onion, sliced
  Handful of celery tops
1 teaspoon salt (for chicken)
3 peppercorns
1 can (15 ounces) pineapple chunks, drained
1 cup diced celery
½ cup slivered almonds
½ cup mayonnaise or salad dressing ,
2 tablespoons milk
¼ teaspoon salt (for salad)
¼ teaspoon dry mustard
⅛ teaspoon pepper
6 Vienna rolls, split and buttered
  Lettuce
  Cherry tomatoes

1 Combine chicken breasts, water, onion, celery tops, 1 teaspoon salt and peppercorns in large saucepan. Simmer, covered, 20 to 30 minutes, or until chicken is tender. Let stand until cool enough to handle, then skin chicken and take meat from bones. Dice chicken (you should have about 2 cups).
2 Combine chicken, pineapple, celery and almonds in medium-size bowl. Mix mayonnaise

or salad dressing, milk, salt, mustard and pepper in 1-cup measure; stir into chicken mixture, tossing lightly to mix; chill until serving time.
3 Line buttered rolls with lettuce; fill with salad mixture, dividing evenly. Top each with 2 or 3 cherry tomatoes.

Chicken Cacciatore Surfers

The traditional cacciatore with a twist—served on hero rolls

Makes 4 servings

4 chicken breasts, weighing about 12 ounces each
4 tablespoons all-purpose flour
1¼ teaspoons salt
¼ teaspoon pepper
¼ cup vegetable oil
4 large ripe tomatoes, diced
½ cup water
2 tablespoons instant minced onion
2 teaspoons sugar
1 teaspoon dry parsley flakes
½ teaspoon leaf basil, crumbled.
4 hero rolls
1 medium-size green pepper, halved, seeded and diced

1 Skin, bone and halve chicken breasts; slice each half to make 2 thin cutlets.
2 Combine flour, salt and pepper in a paper bag; add chicken, a few pieces at a time and coat well; shake off excess flour.
3 Sauté chicken in vegetable oil in a large frying pan, turning to brown on both sides; set chicken aside and keep warm.
4 Add tomatoes, water, onion, sugar, parsley and basil to same pan; simmer, stirring frequently, about 5 minutes. Place chicken over sauce in a single layer. Simmer, uncovered, about 10 minutes, or until chicken is tender and sauce has thickened.
5 Cut a wedge from top of each roll deep enough to hold some sauce. Place 4 pieces of chicken and some of the sauce in rolls; spoon remaining sauce over chicken; sprinkle the tops with diced green pepper.

Galway Stacks

Cabbage roll-ups filled with meat line the hero

Makes 4 servings.

½ medium-size head of cabbage, trimmed and finely shredded (6 cups)
1 can (4 ounces) red chili peppers, drained and chopped
1 medium-size onion, chopped fine (½ cup)
¼ cup cider vinegar
3 tablespoons vegetable oil
¼ cup sugar
1 teaspoon salt
⅛ teaspoon pepper
4 poppy seed rolls
4 tablespoons (½ stick) butter or margarine
2 packages (4 ounces each) sliced corned-beef loaf

1 Place cabbage, chili peppers and onion in a medium-size bowl.

2 Combine vinegar, vegetable oil, sugar, salt and pepper in a cup; stir until sugar dissolves. Pour over cabbage mixture; toss lightly to mix. Let stand, stirring often, at least 1 hour to season; drain well.
3 Split rolls; spread with butter or margarine. Place about ¼ cup of the cabbage mixture on each slice of corned beef; roll up tightly, jelly-roll fashion. Place 3 meat rolls on bottom half of each buttered roll; cover with remaining half.

Stuffed Ham Slices

Cream cheese, Cheddar cheese, celery, onion, and sliced boiled ham fill this roll—which you slice off

Makes 16 servings.

1 loaf unsliced Italian bread (about 18 inches long)

No matter what the preference, if the appetite is there one of these three—**Chicken Cacciatore Surfers, Stuffed Ham Slices,** or **Galway Stacks**—will get 'em.

¼ cup mayonnaise or salad dressing
⅓ cup chopped parsley
1 package (8 ounces) cream cheese
¾ cup very finely chopped celery
½ cup shredded Cheddar cheese
2 tablespoons very finely chopped onion
¼ teaspoon salt
2 packages (4 ounces each) sliced boiled ham
   (8 slices)
1 large dill pickle

1 Split bread; hollow out each half with a fork, leaving a ½-inch-thick shell. (Save insides to make a crumb topping for a casserole.)
2 Spread mayonnaise or salad dressing over hollows in loaf; sprinkle parsley over mayonnaise.
3 Blend cream cheese, celery, Cheddar cheese, onion and salt in a medium-size bowl; spoon into bread halves, packing down well with back of spoon and leaving a small hollow down center.
4 Quarter pickle lengthwise; roll each quarter inside a double-thick slice of ham. Place rolls, end to end, in center of bottom half of loaf; cover with remaining half of bread. Wrap loaf tightly in transparent wrap; chill several hours.
5 To serve, cut into 16 slices. Garnish with parsley sprigs, if you wish.

Stroganoff Subs

Hollow out the inner part of a hero roll and fill with this stroganoff for a delicious treat

Makes 4 servings

1 chuck beefsteak, cut ½ inch thick and
   weighing about 1½ pounds
3 tablespoons butter or margarine
2 envelopes instant beef broth
   OR: 2 teaspoons granulated beef bouillon
2½ cups water
2 tablespoons sliced green onions
1 can (3 or 4 ounces) sliced mushrooms
4 hero rolls
1 tablespoon all-purpose flour
½ cup dairy sour cream

1 Trim fat and bone from steak; cut steak into strips about 1 inch wide and 2 inches long. Brown, half at a time, in part of the butter or margarine in a large frying pan.
2 Stir in beef broth, 2 cups of the water, and green onions. Heat to boiling; cover tightly. Simmer 1½ hours, or until beef is tender. Stir in mushrooms and liquid.

Sliced tomatoes, lettuce, sliced Swiss cheese and ham, make one layer; pickles, cheese, and salami the second layer, in a sesame roll topped with an olive—is what this hero is all about.

3 While meat cooks, cut a thin slice from top of each roll; hollow out insides and set aside with tops to make croutons for another day. Place rolls on a cookie sheet; heat in moderate oven (350°) 10 minutes, or until lightly toasted.
4 Blend flour and remaining ½ cup water until smooth in a cup; stir into meat mixture. Cook, stirring constantly, until mixture thickens and boils 1 minute. *Very slowly* stir in sour cream. (Do not let mixture boil.)
5 Place rolls on serving plates; spoon meat mixture into hollows. Sprinkle with chopped parsley, if you wish. Serve hot.

Super Cheese Hero

Fancy enough for company, but easy on the cook

Makes 1 serving.

1 small sweet red pepper
1 small sweet green pepper
2 teaspoons olive oil
⅛ teaspoon crushed red pepper
⅛ teaspoon leaf basil
⅛ teaspoon oregano
1 French roll
4 thin slices mozzarella cheese
5 anchovy fillets

1 Halve and seed red and green peppers. Cut into thin strips and sauté until crisply tender

(continued)

in olive oil in a small skillet. Sprinkle with crushed red pepper, basil, and oregano. Stir briefly and remove from heat.

2 Cut thin slice from top of French roll. Scoop out soft center from roll. Toast roll under broiler until golden.

3 Spoon pepper mixture into shell; top with mozarrella. Place under broiler to melt cheese.

4 Remove from broiler. Crisscross anchovy fillets over cheese. Place top of roll over all.

Stuffed Salad Rolls

A little salad goes far in these inviting summer sandwiches

Makes 4 servings, 2 rolls each

2 cups chopped lettuce
1 cups diced cooked meat, fish or chicken*
½ cup diced process American or Swiss cheese
½ cup chopped celery
½ cup mayonnaise or salad dressing
2 tablespoons pickle relish
¼ teaspoon curry powder
8 frankfurter rolls, split, toasted and buttered

1 Combine lettuce with meat, fish or chicken, cheese and celery in medium-size bowl.

2 Blend mayonnaise or salad dressing, pickle relish and curry powder in small bowl; stir into salad mixture to coat well; pile into prepared rolls.

* You can use ham, tongue, cold cuts, tuna, shrimps or crabmeat.

Italian-Sausage Heroes

Plump sausages perch atop herb-seasoned vegetables in crisp rolls

Bake at 350° for 10 minutes.
Makes 4 servings.

8 sweet Italian sausages (about 1¼ pounds)
1 Bermuda onion, peeled and chopped
2 large green peppers, quartered, seeded and sliced
1 teaspoon salt
1 teaspoon sugar
1 teaspoon Italian seasoning

Next time you have a group over for a quick bite, fill them up with **Italian-Sausage Heroes.** No one will go away hungry.

2 large tomatoes, chopped
2 large hero rolls
Butter or margarine

1 Score sausages every ½ inch; sauté slowly in a large frying pan 15 minutes, or until cooked through; drain on paper toweling.

2 Pour off all drippings, then measure 3 tablespoons and return to pan; stir in onion and sauté until soft. Stir in peppers, salt, sugar and Italian seasoning; cover; cook 5 minutes.

3 Stir in tomatoes; place sausages on top; cover. Steam 5 minutes, or until mixture is bubbly-hot.

4 While vegetables cook, split hero rolls; cut out center of each half to make a boat-shape shell. (Save centers to use for a crumb topper or croutons.) Spread insides of rolls with butter or margarine; place on a cookie sheet.

5 Heat in moderate oven (350°) 10 minutes or until crispy-hot. Place on serving plates; spoon vegetable mixture into hollows; top each with 2 sausages. Garnish with a quartered stalk of Belgian endive and a radish posy, if you wish. To fix, trim radish, then cut lengthwise into twelfths from root end almost to stem end. Chill in a bowl of ice and water.

Liver-and-Egg Boats

Sliced cucumber and liverwurst, and egg salad make the double fillings for hotdog rolls

Makes 4 servings.

4 hard-cooked eggs, shelled
½ cup mayonnaise or salad dressing
¼ cup chopped parsley
  Salt and pepper
4 split frankfurter rolls
4 leaves romaine
8 slices liverwurst (about ½ pound)
½ medium-size cucumber, pared and cut in 16 slices

1 Press eggs through a sieve or mash with a fork in a small bowl; blend in ¼ cup of the mayonnaise or salad dressing, chopped parsley and salt and pepper to taste.
2 Spread frankfurter rolls with remaining ¼ cup mayonnaise or salad dressing; top half of each with a romaine leaf, then egg salad.
3 Arrange liverwurst and cucumber slices, alternately, on remaining halves of rolls. Sprinkle egg salad with paprika and garnish liverwurst with parsley, if you wish.

Whopper Heroes

Pile meat, cheese, egg and tomato slices on split French bread, then let everyone cut off a "sandwich."

Makes 6 to 9 servings

3 loaves French bread
¾ cup mayonnaise or salad dressing
3 tablespoons prepared mustard
  Lettuce
2 pounds cold cuts (such as spiced ham, swiss cheese, liverwurst, salami, American cheese, corned beef, boiled ham)
3 hard cooked eggs
2 tomatoes, sliced
1 onion, sliced
1 green pepper, sliced
  Olive oil
  Pickled yellow wax peppers
  Pickled sweet red peppers

1 Split French breads in half; spread generously with a mixture of mayonnaise or salad dressing and prepared mustard.
2 Cover bottom halves of bread with lettuce;

(continued)

Both kids and adults enjoy surprises, and everyone loves a hero. So set out a giant loaf of French or Italian bread and stack with as many different kinds of meats and cheeses, and let each person choose a hero—and cut off—as in the **Whopper Heroes.**

place folded slices of spiced ham, Swiss cheese, liverwurst, salami, process American cheese, corned beef and boiled ham on top. (Or choose your own favorite cold cuts and cheeses.)

3 Tuck slices of hard-cooked egg, tomato, onion and red and green pepper between meats; drizzle lightly with olive oil for a real Italian touch.

4 Garnish with pickled yellow wax peppers and pickled sweet red peppers threaded onto long wooden picks, kebab style, and a bow of red- and green-pepper strips. To serve, set kebabs aside; cover filling with spread top of bread; cut in half or thirds crosswise.

All-American Hero

Potato salad, sardines, tomatoes and pickles go into this whopper of a sandwich

Makes 6 servings

2 cups diced, peeled, cooked potatoes
¾ cup chopped celery
1 small onion, chopped (¼ cup)
¼ pound (half an 8-ounce package) process American cheese, cut into small cubes
2 hard-cooked eggs, shelled and chopped
1 teaspoon salt
¼ teaspoon pepper

½ cup mayonnaise or salad dressing
1 teaspoon prepared mustard
1 long loaf French bread, split lengthwise and buttered
2 cans (about 4 ounces each) sardines, drained
2 dill pickles, sliced thin lengthwise
1 tomato, sliced thin

1 Combine potatoes, celery, onion, cheese, eggs, salt and pepper in medium-size bowl; fold in mayonnaise or salad dressing and mustard until well blended.

2 Pile potato salad on bottom half of buttered bread; arrange sardines and pickle and tomato slices in layers on top; replace top crust. Slice crosswise into 6 servings

East-West Tuna Whoppers

Filled-to-the-brim whoppers, topped with a sauce that tastes of the Orient

Makes 4 servings.

1 package (7 ounces) frozen Chinese pea pods
1 can (1 pound) chop suey vegetables
3 tablespoons cornstarch
¾ teaspoon ground ginger
1 tablespoon soy sauce
2 tablespoons butter or margarine

4 sesame-seed buns, split and toasted
2 cans tuna (about 7 ounces each), drained and broken into small chunks
1 bunch green onions, trimmed and sliced (about ⅓ cup)

1 Cook pea pods, following label directions; drain liquid into a 2-cup measure. Drain liquid from vegetables into same measure; add water, if needed, to make 1½ cups.
2 Mix cornstarch and ginger in a medium-size saucepan; stir in the 1½ cups vegetable liquid and soy sauce until smooth. Cook, stirring constantly, until sauce thickens and boils 3 minutes.
3 Stir in pea pods, vegetables and butter or margarine; heat slowly to boiling.
4 Place buns, cut sides up, on serving plates; spoon part of the sauce mixture over buns; top with tuna, then remaining sauce. Sprinkle sliced green onions over all. Serve immediately and accompany with knife and fork.

Provençal Pan Bagna

Also called "pan bagnat" or "pain baigné," the name means "bathed bread" as the bread is bathed in olive oil for flavor

Makes 4 servings.

4 hard-crusted French rolls or hero rolls
½ cup olive oil

2 tablespoons red wine vinegar
2 cloves garlic, minced
¼ teaspoon leaf basil, crumbled
2 medium-size tomatoes, halved and thinly sliced
1 small green pepper, halved, seeded and cut into thin strips
1 small red onion, sliced and separated into rings
Salt
Pepper
4 hard-cooked eggs, sliced
1 can (2 ounces) flat anchovy fillets, drained (12)
10 pitted ripe olives, halved

1 Cut rolls in half horizontally. Combine oil, vinegar, garlic and basil in a 1-cup measure; stir until blended. Drizzle 1 tablespoon mixture on each cut side of rolls.
2 Arrange tomato slices on bottom halves of rolls, overlapping to fit; top with green pepper strips and onion rings. Sprinkle with salt and pepper. Arrange egg slices over onion rings; top with anchovy fillets and olives. Sprinkle with more salt and pepper; drizzle with any leftover dressing.
3 Carefully place tops of rolls over filled bottoms; press down gently. The flavor of these sandwiches improves on standing a short while. For picnics, wrap in foil or plastic.

A crunchy shell and a fish flavor characterize this meal-in-one hero, the **Provençal Pan Bagna.**

Western Tuna Buns

This happy combination of tastes will bring you a hatful of compliments

Makes 8 servings.

1 can (about 7 ounces) tuna, drained and flaked
1 can (about 8 ounces) pineapple chunks, drained
½ cup finely diced celery
¼ cup finely diced green pepper
¼ cup toasted slivered almonds
¼ cup mayonnaise or salad dressing
½ teaspoon salt
⅛ teaspoon pepper
1 teaspoon lemon juice
8 hamburger rolls, split, toasted and buttered
Romaine or Boston lettuce

1 Combine tuna, pineapple, celery, green pepper, almonds, mayonnaise or salad dressing, salt, pepper and lemon juice in bowl; mix lightly.
2 Line hamburger rolls with romaine or lettuce; fill with salad mixture; wrap each in a paper napkin for easy eating.

Oven Tuna Buns

This sandwich is served hot—for a different taste, serve it cold and accompany with a hot drink

Bake at 350° for 25 minutes.
Makes 4 servings

2 cans (about 7 ounces each) tuna, drained and flaked
1 package (3 or 4 ounces) cream cheese, cut in small cubes
6 water chestnuts, drained and chopped
2 tablespoons finely cut chives
2 tablespoons chopped parsley
⅓ cup mayonnaise or salad dressing
2 tablespoons chili sauce
4 large poppy-seed rolls

1 Combine tuna, cream cheese, water chestnuts, chives and parsley in a medium-size bowl.
2 Blend mayonnaise or salad dressing and chili sauce in a cup; fold into tuna mixture.
3 Cut a thin slice from top of each roll; hollow

out inside, leaving a ¼-inch-thick shell. Spoon tuna mixture into hollows, dividing evenly; set tops of rolls back in place. Wrap each sandwich in foil; place on a cookie sheet.
4 Bake in moderate oven (350°) 25 minutes. Unwrap; serve hot.

Hot Crab Salad Boats

Rolls are buttery-crisp; filling is refreshing and just hearty enough for summer eating.

Bake at 400° for 15 minutes.
Makes 6 servings

2 packages (about 6 ounces each) frozen Alaska king crabmeat, thawed and drained
1 cup chopped celery
1 cup frozen green peas
¼ pound (half an 8-ounce package) process Swiss cheese, cut into small cubes
¼ cup chopped parsley
¾ cup mayonnaise or salad dressing
6 long hero rolls
4 tablespoons (½ stick) butter or margarine, melted

1 Cut crabmeat into bite-size pieces, carefully removing any thin bony tissue. Combine with celery, peas, cheese and parsley in medium-size bowl; mix in mayonnaise or salad dressing.
2 Cut off a slice across top of each roll; cut out middle with a sharp knife to make a boat-shape shell. (Save tops and middle pieces to make toasty croutons.) Brush inside of shells with melted butter or margarine; fill with crabmeat mixture. Wrap each separately in foil.
3 Bake in hot oven (400°) 15 minutes, or just until filling is hot. Thread a lemon wedge and 2 ripe olives onto a wooden pick to serve with each sandwich, if you wish.

Greek Gyro

In Greek or Near Eastern restaurants, this sandwich is made with well-seasoned lamb cooked on a slowly rotating vertical spit: as the outer surface of the meat browns, slivers of flavorful hot lamb are cut off

Makes 6 servings.

1 pound ground lean leg of lamb
1 cup fresh bread crumbs (2 slices)

A meal from the sea is easy when you team Alaska king crab, frozen peas, Swiss cheese, celery, parsley, and mayonnaise in **Hot Crab Salad Boats.**

2 tablespoons chopped parsley
1 large clove garlic, finely chopped
1 teaspoon salt
1 teaspoon chili powder
½ teaspoon ground cumin
¼ teaspoon finely ground fenugreek seeds
  Dash cayenne pepper
6 rounds pita bread
1 small onion
½ cup dairy sour cream
½ teaspoon dried dill
  OR: 1½ teaspoons chopped fresh dillweed
½ teaspoon salt
2 teaspoons lemon juice
1 medium-size tomato
3 cups shredded lettuce
  Lemon
  Dill

1 Combine lamb, bread crumbs, parsley, garlic, the 1 teaspoon salt, chili, cumin, fenugreek and cayenne in a large bowl. Mix very well with spoon or with hands.

2 Shape lamb into 4x6-inch patty about 1 inch thick. Broil, turning once, until well browned on each side, about 15 minutes. Remove lamb from broiler and let rest 10 minutes before slicing. Wrap pita in foil; place in hot oven to warm when lamb is removed.

3 Meanwhile, cut onion from top to bottom into julienne strips. Place in bowl with sour cream, dill, the ½ teaspoon salt and lemon juice; stir until mixed. Slice tomato from top to bottom; cut slices into halves.

4 Cut lamb lengthwise into thin strips. Remove pita from foil; fold each pita in half across the

(continued)

A refreshing blend of lamb, garlic, chili powder, sour cream, tomatoes, and shredded lettuce make **Greek Gyro** a foreign version of a hero.

An attractive combination of pita bread, Feta cheese, shredded lettuce, cucumbers, and tomatoes, and yogurt makes **Mediterranean Salad Sandwich** a welcome meal-in-one.

center; fill each with some strips of lamb, shredded lettuce, sliced tomatoes and sour cream-onion mixture. For easier eating, wrap one end

of each in plastic wrap and, if you wish, overwrap with napkin. Garnish with lemon wedges and dill.

Mediterranean Salad Sandwich

A cheese hero with a Greek twist

Makes 1 serving.

    1 round pita bread
    4 half-inch slices Feta cheese
      Lettuce, shredded
    1 small cucumber, diced
    1 tomato, diced
 ¼ cup plain yogurt
    1 clove garlic
    1 tablespoon chopped parsley
      Milk
    1 green onion

1 Heat round of pita. Cut in half.
2 Fill each half with 2 slices Feta, shredded lettuce, cucumber, and tomato.
3 Combine yogurt, crushed garlic, chopped parsley. Thin with milk and spoon over filling. Garnish with green onion.

It's a lucky person who bites into **Swiss and Sprout Sandwich Special.** The soft blending of flavors is both a surprise and a delight.

OLD-TIME FAVORITES

Swiss and Sprout Sandwich Special

A change of pace that's bound to please

Makes 1 serving.

2 slices pumpernickel bread
Butter
2 slices Swiss cheese
Spinach leaves, washed
Tomato
Red onion, sliced
½ cup alfalfa sprouts, washed and drained
Mayonnaise or salad dressing

1 Butter pumpernickel. On one slice layer the Swiss cheese, a few spinach leaves, two thin slices of tomato and some red onion rings.
2 Mix alfalfa sprouts with 1 tablespoon finely chopped red onion and just enough mayonnaise or salad dressing to moisten.
3 Place alfalfa sprout mixture on top of sandwich and cover with remaining bread slice.

Pocketbook Hotdogs

Accompany these spellbinders with a green salad or a tart dessert

Bake biscuits at 450° for 12 minutes.
Makes 4 servings

2 cups biscuit mix
Milk
1 cup shredded process American cheese
4 frankfurters
4 slices bacon, cooked and crumbled
2 tablespoons butter or margarine
2 tablespoons prepared mustard

1 Prepare biscuit mix with milk, following label directions for rolled biscuits; stir in ⅓ cup of the cheese.
2 Turn dough out onto a lightly floured pastry cloth or board; knead several times, or until smooth. Pat out to a rectangle, 6x5; cut crosswise into 4 pieces. Place on a cookie sheet.
3 Bake in very hot oven (450°) 12 minutes, or until golden. Remove from oven; raise temperature to BROIL.
4 While biscuits bake, heat frankfurters in water, following label directions; drain. Mix remaining cheese and bacon in a small bowl.

(continued)

5 Split biscuits lengthwise almost through; spread with butter or margarine, then mustard. Place a frankfurter in each biscuit; sprinkle with bacon mixture. Return to cookie sheet.
6 Broil, 4 to 5 inches from heat, 1 minute, or until cheese melts. Serve hot.

Deep-Sea Stacks

As simple as layering tuna salad between crisp cucumbers on bread spread with curry butter

Makes 4 servings

6 *tablespoons (¾ stick) butter or margarine*
½ *teaspoon curry powder*
8 *slices bread*
1 *can (about 7 ounces) tuna, drained and flaked*
¼ *cup mayonnaise or salad dressing*
 Salt and pepper
1 *medium-size cucumber, pared and sliced thin*

1 Blend butter and curry powder in small bowl; spread on bread slices.
2 Combine tuna and mayonnaise or salad dressing in small bowl; season with salt and pepper.

3 Layer each of 4 slices of bread this way: Cucumber slices, tuna mixture and cucumber slices, dividing evenly. Top with remaining bread slices, butter side down.
4 Slice each in half crosswise; garnish with carrot curls, if you wish.

Cream Cheese-Date-Nut Sandwich

A sweet delight that's perfect for easy entertaining

Makes 1 serving.

1 *tablespoon honey*
1 *package (3 ounces) cream cheese*
⅓ *cup chopped dates*
¼ *cup chopped walnuts*
 Raisin bread
1 *red apple*
 Mint (optional)

1 Beat honey into softened cream cheese.
2 Add chopped dates and walnuts; mix well.
3 Spread thickly on slices of raisin bread; serve with wedges of apple. Garnish with mint if you wish.

Don't settle for the ordinary, just because you have a plate of sandwiches on the table. Choose a special bread and a delicious filling as with **Cream Cheese-Date-Nut Sandwich.**

You don't always have to be imaginative to please both the young and the old. And here is a good example. A peanut butter and jelly sandwich rarely finds no takers.

Stuffed Ham Slices

A crusty loaf with a ham-cheese-pickle core

Makes 16 servings.

1 loaf unsliced Italian bread (about 18 inches long)
¼ cup mayonnaise or salad dressing
⅓ cup chopped parsley
8 ounces cream cheese
¾ cup very finely chopped celery
2 tablespoons very finely chopped onion
¼ teaspoon salt
2 packages (4 ounces each) sliced boiled ham
1 large dill pickle

1 Split bread lengthwise; hollow out each half with a fork, leaving a ½-inch-thick shell. (Save insides to make a crumb topping for a casserole.)
2 Spread mayonnaise or salad dressing over hollows in loaf; sprinkle parsley over mayonnaise or salad dressing.
3 Blend cream cheese, celery, onion and salt in a bowl; spoon into bread halves, packing down well and leaving a small hollow down center.
4 Quarter pickle lengthwise; roll each quarter inside a double-thick slice of ham. Place rolls, end to end, in center of bottom half of loaf;

cover with remaining half of bread. Wrap tightly; chill.
5 To serve, cut into 16 slices. Garnish with parsley.

Bavarian Beef Plate

Relishlike sauerkraut tops corned beef and cheese on zesty pumpernickel

Makes 4 servings

1 can (1 pound) sauerkraut, well drained and chopped
½ cup bottled Thousand Island dressing
8 large slices pumpernickel, buttered
1 package (8 ounces) sliced Muenster cheese
1 can (12 ounces) corned beef, cut into 8 slices
Dill pickles, sliced
Spiced crab apples

1 Mix sauerkraut and Thousand Island dressing in a small bowl.
2 Place 1 slice of bread on each of 4 serving plates; top each with cheese, then corned beef.
3 Spoon sauerkraut mixture over corned beef; cover with remaining slices of bread. Hold in place with wooden picks topped with pickle slices. Cut each sandwich in half. Garnish plates with spiced crab apples.

SANDWICHES YOU CAN FREEZE

- *Ground roast beef, lamb, pork, ham, veal, or chicken, moistened with mayonnaise or catsup and seasoned with grated onion or Worcestershire sauce.*
- *Chopped cooked chicken livers or calf or lamb liver mixed with mashed hard-cooked egg yolk, minced onion, and catsup.*
- *Cream cheese, chopped stuffed olives, and salted peanuts, moistened with undiluted evaporated milk.*
- *Mashed sardines, lemon juice, grated onion.*
- *Sliced roast lamb, on bread spread with mint-seasoned butter (1 stick [¼ pound] butter or margarine creamed with 1 tablespoon chopped fresh mint).*
- *Peanut butter and honey; peanut butter and crisp bacon bits; peanut butter and applesauce; peanut butter and sliced sweet pickle.*
- *Canned corned beef or liver-spread seasoned with grated onion, chopped pickle, or chili sauce.*
- *Chopped hard-cooked egg yolks, crisp bacon bits, grated onion, catsup.*
- *Deviled ham, chopped mustard pickle, mashed hard-cooked egg yolks.*
- *Ground cooked ham, ground Cheddar cheese, minced onion, chili sauce.*
- *Canned tuna, on bread spread with savory butter (1 stick [¼ pound] butter or margarine creamed with 2 tablespoons catsup, mustard-pickle relish, or tomato-pickle relish).*
- *Chopped cooked chicken, chopped salted almonds, and cream cheese, softened with milk.*

Rivieras

Ham and chicken, French-toasted, with mayonnaise-cranberry sauce to top it off

Makes 6 servings.

½ cup (1 stick) butter or margarine
12 half-inch-thick slices French bread
12 slices cooked chicken
 1 package (6 ounces) sliced boiled ham
 3 eggs
¾ cup milk
 1 cup mayonnaise or salad dressing
 1 can (8 ounces) whole-fruit cranberry sauce

1 Spread half of the butter or margarine on bread; make into 6 sandwiches with chicken and ham, dividing evenly.
2 Beat eggs slightly with milk in a pie plate; dip sandwiches into mixture, turning to coat both sides well. Brown slowly in remaining butter or margarine, turning once, in a large frying pan.
3 Blend mayonnaise or salad dressing with cranberry sauce in a small bowl. Serve sandwiches hot with dressing.

Barbecue Bunburgers

Quick contents: Barbecue filling from a can, cheese from a package

Heat rolls at 400° for 10 minutes, bake sandwiches at 400° for 5 minutes.
Makes 6 servings.

6 oblong hard rolls
1 large onion, peeled and sliced
1 large green pepper, seeded and diced
4 tablespoons (½ stick) butter or margarine
1 can (about 1 pound) barbecue sauce with beef
1 package (8 ounces) sliced process American cheese, cut in strips
2 cups shredded iceberg lettuce

1 Cut a thin slice from tops, then hollow out rolls. Place rolls and tops on a cookie sheet. Heat in hot oven (400°) 10 minutes, or until toasted.
2 Sauté onion and green pepper in butter or margarine until soft in a medium-size frying pan; stir in beef mixture; heat until bubbly. Spoon into hollows in rolls; top with cheese strips.
3 Bake in hot oven (400°) 5 minutes, or until cheese melts. Cover each with shredded lettuce and top of roll. Serve hot.

Chicken Jumbos

Chicken teams with green beans to make this sandwich doubly good

Makes 4 servings.

8 slices whole-wheat bread
½ cup prepared sandwich spread
 Lettuce
8 slices cooked chicken
1 can (about 1 pound) whole Blue Lake green beans, drained

Sweet pickle slices
Ripe olives

1 Spread bread with sandwich spread. (Butter first, if you wish.)
2 Layer each of 4 slices this way: Lettuce, chicken, and green beans, dividing evenly. Top with remaining bread, sandwich-spread side down.
3 Cut each in half crosswise: garnish with sweet pickle slices and ripe olives threaded on a wooden pick.

Give 'em a choice, and they'll generally be satisfied. And this is never more true than when you serve up **Barbecue Bunburgers** and **Rivieras.**

For a nutritious, satisfying lunch, have a full-bodied soup, milk, fruit, and a peanut butter and lettuce sandwich.

Beef Roll-Ups

These sandwiches offer all kinds of ingredients

Makes 6 servings.

8 ounces cream cheese, softened
1 envelope (.7 ounces) onion salad dressing mix
1 tablespoon prepared horseradish
1 to 2 tablespoons milk
18 thin slices roast beef
12 thin carrot sticks
12 large slices dark rye bread
¼ cup (½ stick) butter or margarine, softened
6 lettuce leaves
6 slices Swiss cheese

1 Blend cream cheese, salad dressing mix, horseradish and milk in a medium-size bowl. Spread about 1 tablespoon of the mixture on each roast beef slice. Place a carrot stick at one end of each roast beef slice; roll, jelly-roll fashion: set aside.

2 Butter bread slices and then layer 6 of them with lettuce leaves, Swiss cheese and beef roll-ups (3 on each slice). Top with remaining 6 slices bread. Cut each in half; wrap, chill, or serve immediately.

Zigzag Sandwich Loaf

Spice this one by first coating the cut slices with garlic butter

Bake at 425° for 15 minutes.
Makes 6 servings

1 loaf French bread
¼ cup melted butter or margarine

2 tablespoons pickle relish
1 tablespoon prepared mustard
12 slices (about ½ pound) bologna
¼ pound process American cheese, cut in 1-
    inch strips

1 Cut bread diagonally into 6 thick slices almost through to bottom crust; turn loaf end for end; slice same way again to make zigzag cuts completely across top.
2 Combine melted butter or margarine, pickle relish and mustard; brush between slices; fill cuts in bread with folded bologna slices and cheese strips (have cheese overlap crust so it will melt over top); wrap loaf loosely in aluminum foil; seal.
3 Bake in hot oven (425°) 10 minutes; open foil wrapper and fold back; bake 5 minutes longer, or until cheese is golden-brown and slightly melted. Serve hot.

ROBUST CLUBS AND DAGWOODS

Grilled Seafood Cheese Stacks

Tuna and shrimp are the surprise ingredients

Bake at 400° for 10 to 12 minutes.
Makes 6 servings

 1 can (about 7 ounces) tuna, drained and
    flaked
 1 package (5 ounces) frozen deveined cooked
    shrimps, thawed
 ½ cup diced celery
 1 pimiento, cut in thin strips
 ¼ teaspoon salt
 ⅛ teaspoon pepper
 ½ cup dairy sour cream
 ¼ cup mayonnaise or salad dressing
18 slices bread
 ¼ cup (½ stick) melted butter or margarine
 3 tomatoes, sliced
 2 tablespoons grated onion
 ¼ pound (1 cup) grated sharp Cheddar cheese

1 Combine tuna, shrimps, celery, pimiento, salt, pepper, sour cream and mayonnaise or salad dressing in medium-size bowl; mix lightly.
2 Trim crusts from sliced bread; brush with

melted butter or margarine; put together to make 6 three-decker sandwiches with tuna-shrimp mixture for one filling, tomato slices and grated onion for the second; sprinkle tops with grated cheese; place on cookie sheet.
3 Bake in hot oven (400°) 10 to 12 minutes, or until cheese melts.

All-American Club

The aristocrat of sandwiches—a three-decker of buttery toast with meat, cheese and tomato

Makes 6 servings

12 slices white or whole-wheat bread, toasted
    and buttered
    Lettuce
 8 slices ripe tomatoes
12 slices (about ½ pound) bacon, crisply
    cooked
 4 slices cooked ham
 4 slices process Swiss cheese
    Prepared mustard or mayonnaise
    Stuffed olives
    Sweet gherkins

1 Arrange 4 slices buttered toast in a row; top each with lettuce, 2 slices tomato and 3 strips bacon; add a second slice of toast, then lettuce and a slice each of ham and cheese.
2 Spread remaining toast with mustard or mayonnaise; lay, spread side down, on top of cheese; insert 4 wooden picks into each sandwich to hold it together; cut each diagonally into 4 triangles; stick olives and gherkins onto ends of wooden picks.

Chicken-Cheese Clubs

Tomatoes and crisp cucumber make relishlike partners for bacon, chicken and Muenster

Bake at 450° for 5 minutes.
Makes 4 servings.

12 slices bacon (½ pound)
 2 medium-size tomatoes, each cut in 4 slices
 ½ small cucumber, sliced
12 slices whole-wheat bread, toasted and but-
    tered
 ¼ cup prepared sandwich spread
 8 slices cooked chicken
 4 slices Muenster cheese (from an 8-ounce
    package)
 8 pitted ripe olives
 8 small sweet pickles

(continued)

1 Sauté bacon until crisp in a large frying pan; drain on paper toweling.
2 Place tomato and cucumber slices and bacon, dividing evenly, on 4 pieces of the toast; add another slice of toast; spread with sandwich spread.
3 Top with chicken slices, then cheese and remaining toast, buttered side down. Place sandwiches on a cookie sheet.
4 Bake in very hot oven (450°) 5 minutes, or until cheese melts slightly.
5 Press wooden picks into sandwiches to hold in place; cut each sandwich diagonally into quarters. Top picks with olives and pickles.

Tomato Clubs

Build this triple-deck "sandwich-salad" of thick juicy tomato slices with lots of meat and cheese between

Makes 4 servings

```
 4  large tomatoes
1½  teaspoons sugar
1½  teaspoons salt
 ¼  teaspoon pepper
 4  slices process Swiss cheese (from an 8-
    ounce package)
 8  slices white bread
    Mayonnaise or salad dressing
    Leaf lettuce
 8  slices cooked chicken, turkey or ham
 8  slices crisp bacon
    Stuffed green and ripe olives
    Bottled blue-cheese salad dressing
```

1 Peel tomatoes and cut out stem ends; cut each into 3 thick slices, keeping slices in order.
2 Combine sugar, salt and pepper in a cup. Cut cheese slices into ¼-inch-wide strips.
3 Toast bread; trim crusts, then spread toast with mayonnaise or salad dressing. Halve 4 slices diagonally; place 1 whole slice and 2 halves on either side on each of 4 serving plates as a base for "sandwiches."
4 Build each this way: Place stem end slice of tomato, cut side up, on toast; sprinkle with seasoning mixture; top with lettuce, chicken,

Vary a club and you vary the pleasure. The traditional club calls for three pieces of bread, or toast, and two kinds of fillings. In making **Tomato Clubs,** the bread becomes a base for layers of tomato slices, meat and cheese.

turkey or ham slices, tomato slice, more seasoning mixture, lettuce, cheese strips, bacon, remaining tomato slice and any remaining seasoning mixture.
5 Hold together with a long wooden pick threaded with green and ripe olives. Serve with blue-cheese dressing or with your favorite mayonnaise or salad dressing, if you wish.

Bacon-Spinach Junior Club Sandwiches

The flavor of this sandwich is reminiscent of the popular sweet-sour spinach salad with chopped egg and bacon bits: called a "junior club," it consists of two slices of bread rather than the usual three

Makes 4 servings.

```
12  slices bacon
 4  eggs
 1  medium-size onion, finely chopped (½ cup)
 ½  cup mayonnaise or salad dressing
 2  tablespoons red wine vinegar
 1  tablespoon sugar
 ½  teaspoon salt
    Dash pepper
 8  slices firm white bread, toasted
    Spinach leaves
12  cherry tomatoes
    Green onions
```

1 Fry bacon until crisp in large skillet; drain on paper toweling. Remove all but about ¼ cup fat from pan. Break eggs, 1 at a time, into hot fat; fry until firm, breaking yolks with a pancake turner, and turning them over. Transfer to warm platter. Remove and discard all but 1 tablespoon of the fat from pan.
2 Cook onion in remaining fat until tender. Remove from heat. Stir in mayonnaise or salad dressing, vinegar, sugar, salt and pepper.
3 Spread mayonnaise mixture on each slice of toast. Cover four slices with a layer of spinach leaves, 3 slices bacon, a fried egg and top with more spinach leaves. Cover with remaining slices of toast, mayonnaise-coated side down. With serrated knife, cut sandwiches into 4 triangles.
4 Alternately spear triangles with cherry tomatoes on 8-inch skewers. Serve on platter garnished with a tomato poppy and green onion brushes, if you wish. To make garnish, take 2 cherry tomatoes; cut one not quite through into 4 wedges, the other into 6 wedges. Remove pulp. Place the 6-petaled tomato inside the 4-
(continued)

petaled tomato. Cut a ½-inch piece of the white part of a green onion at the end into crisscross slashes. Spread end out and put in center of tomato poppy. For green onion brushes, use 5-inch onions and cut green part into lengthwise shreds about 1 inch long.

Ham-and-Egg Towers

Six layers of bread are filled with ham and egg salad, then frosted with cream cheese

Makes 8 servings.

    6 hard-cooked eggs, shelled and chopped
    ½ cup diced celery
    ½ cup mayonnaise or salad dressing
    ½ teaspoon prepared mustard
    ½ teaspoon salt
    1 cup ground cooked ham
    2 packages (8 ounces each) cream cheese,
         softened
    6 tablespoons light cream or table cream
   12 slices round white bread
    ½ cup chopped parsley

1 Mix chopped eggs, celery, mayonnaise or salad dressing, mustard and salt in a medium-size bowl.
2 Blend ground ham, half of one package of the cream cheese, and 1 tablespoon of the cream until smooth in a small bowl. Place remaining cream cheese and cream in a medium-size bowl; set aside for Step 4.
3 Spread egg-salad mixture on 6 slices of the bread and ham on 4 slices. Stack slices, alternating egg with ham, in 2 piles of 5 each; top with remaining bread slices.
4 Blend cream cheese and cream in bowl until smooth; spread over each sandwich stack to frost completely. Pat parsley on tops and sides to cover. Chill several hours.
5 When ready to serve, cut each stack into quarters with a very sharp knife. Garnish with dill-pickle wheels and serve with radish roses, if you wish. To make dill-pickle wheels, shave thin strips from medium-size dill pickles with a vegetable parer. Roll strips, then bunch 3 together; wrap another strip around all to hold them in place.

Cheddar Club Sandwich

A change from the usual club, this one is made with two kinds of bread

Makes 1 sandwich.

    3 slices bacon
    1 slice whole wheat bread

When company calls on a Sunday night, serve these **Bacon-Spinach Junior Club Sandwiches**— there's not too much effort to put them together, but there's plenty of biteable flavor.

Reward the first person who realizes that **Ham-and-Egg Towers** is not angel food cake but a delicious combination of ham and egg between white bread slices.

2 slices white bread
1 tablespoon mayonnaise or salad dressing
 Lettuce
 Sliced tomato
 Pickle rounds

1 Cook 3 slices bacon until crisp.
2 Toast 1 slice whole wheat bread and 2 slices white bread.
3 Spread slices with mayonnaise, then layer as follows: white toast; slice of Cheddar; bacon; lettuce; slice of whole wheat bread, mayonnaise or salad dressing side up; tomato; lettuce; slice of Cheddar and remaining slice of white bread, mayonnaise or salad dressing side down.
4 Fasten with wooden picks. Cut into 4 tri-
5 Serve with pickle rounds. Garnish with parsley, if you wish.

Club Tower

Triple-deck sandwiches always make a hit. Filling calls for liverwurst, minced ham and chicken or turkey.

Makes 6 servings

12 slices square white bread
 6 slices square whole-wheat bread
 Butter or margarine
 1 jar (5 ounces) smoky cheese spread
 Leaf lettuce
 1 package (6 ounces) sliced liverwurst
 1 package (6 ounces) sliced minced ham
 3 medium-size tomatoes, sliced thin
 1 package (5 ounces) sliced chicken or turkey
 1 bunch radishes, trimmed
 2 cans (about 2 ounces each) potato sticks

1 Toast bread. Spread white slices with butter or margarine and whole-wheat slices with cheese spread.
2 Layer each of 6 slices white toast this way: Lettuce; liverwurst; minced ham; whole-wheat toast, cheese side up; tomato slices; chicken or turkey; white toast, buttered side down. Hold in place with wooden picks; place on serving plates. Garnish with radishes.
3 Cut each sandwich diagonally into 4 triangles. Serve with potato sticks.

When you arrange for the next bridge game, let your guests know that once the bidding is done with you'll serve **Cheddar Club Sandwiches.**

SOME SANDWICH-MAKING TIPS

• *For variety, take advantage of all the inviting flavors and shapes of breads, rolls and buns that are available today. And once in a while put some fun in your job and the lunch box, too, by using two kinds of bread for a sandwich—whole wheat and white, or white and rye, for example. Just be sure to choose slices of the same size and shape so the edges will fit together neatly.*

• *To keep fillings from soaking into the bread, spread the butter or margarine all the way to the crusts.*

• *For easy spreading without tearing bread, always soften regular or whipped butter or margarine first, or depend on soft margarine. Another trick is to freeze the bread first; then the butter spreads like a dream.*

• *No need to trim the crusts from bread except on the daintiest sandwiches. Crusts will help keep the edges of the bread from drying out and curling.*

• *For speed when you're making a big batch of sandwiches, use the assembly-line technique; that is, line up the bread slices, two by two, in rows on your counter top, keeping them in order as they come from the loaf.*

• *When making sandwiches "to go," pack lettuce and cucumber slices so they'll stay crisp and fresh: wrap them loosely in wet paper toweling, then bundle into a transparent sandwich bag. Come lunchtime, they can be added to the sandwich. Raw relishes also travel neatly in a transparent bag.*

• *For easy eating, cut sandwiches for youngsters into 4 small wedges, squares or strips.*

• *Set aside a shelf in your cupboard to hold lunch-packing materials—wax paper, foil, transparent wrap and bags and paper napkins; a variety of containers and cups in various sizes and shapes; and plastic knives, forks and spoons. They'll all save you steps and time when you're rushed; some are a help in keeping foods neat and making toting easy.*

DANISH AND OPEN-FACE SANDWICHES

Danish Beef Sandwiches

Cook a big roast so you'll have enough left to turn into these open-face huskies

Makes 4 servings.

4 tablespoons (½ stick) butter or margarine
2 tablespoons prepared horseradish
4 slices pumpernickel bread
12 thin slices roast beef
1 jar (1 pound) sliced pickled beets, drained

1 Blend butter or margarine with horseradish in a small bowl; spread on bread slices.
2 Top each with a slice of beef, then a layer of beets; repeat to make 2 more layers of each. Garnish with parsley and serve with freshly ground pepper, if you wish.

Smorgasbord Sandwiches

This sandwich has everything: rye bread, tongue, caraway and blue cheeses, sardines, hard-cooked eggs and beets

Makes 4 servings

8 slices thin light rye bread, buttered
Iceberg lettuce
1 package (6 ounces) sliced cooked tongue
4 long slices caraway cheese (from an 8-ounce package), folded
4 cherry tomatoes, halved
Watercress
1 can (about 4 ounces) sardines, drained
2 hard-cooked eggs, shelled and sliced
2 wedges (about 1 ounce each) blue cheese, crumbled
1 jar (about 1 pound) sliced pickled beets, drained
1 can (about 4 ounces) French fried onions

1 Place 1 slice rye bread on each of 4 serving plates. Halve remaining 4 slices diagonally; arrange each 2 triangles around whole slices on plates; top all with several leaves of lettuce.
2 Layer tongue and cheese slices, cherry tomatoes and watercress on top of whole slices of bread. Place sardines on one of the triangles on each plate, and hard-cooked egg slices on the other; sprinkle crumbled blue cheese over eggs.

A open face sandwich doesn't have to be just a slice of bread with a slice of cheese or left-over meat, as this attractive-looking, mouth-watering selection shows.

3 Spoon beets into lettuce cups at one side of sandwiches; sprinkle lightly with dillweed, if you wish, and serve with French fried onions.

Ham-and-Caraway Foldovers

For these typically Danish open-facers, pile meat and cheese on zesty rye

Makes 4 servings

3 tablespoons butter or margarine.
½ teaspoon prepared mustard
4 slices square rye bread

2 packages (6 ounces each) sliced boiled ham
4 slices caraway cheese (from an 8-ounce package)
DILLED CUCUMBER CRISPS (recipe follows)

1 Blend butter or margarine with mustard in a cup; spread on bread.
2 Fold ham and cheese slices; pile on top of bread. Garnish with DILLED CUCUMBER CRISPS and a sprig of fresh dill, if you wish.

DILLED CUCUMBER CRISPS
Combine ¼ cup cider vinegar, 2 tablespoons sugar and 1 teaspoon chopped fresh dill in a small bowl; stir until sugar dissolves. Add ½ thinly sliced small cucumber; toss lightly to mix. Chill at least an hour to season.

Arrange your next buffet sandwich table around this tremendous twosome—**Ham-and-Caraway Foldovers** and **Sun-Glow Salad.**

Sun-Glow Salad

Dollop of apricot-pecan cream tops sweet-sour carrot relish on pumpernickel bread

Makes 4 servings

4 medium-size carrots, pared and grated
1 tablespoon honey
1 tablespoon lemon juice
½ cup cream for whipping
1 teaspoon sugar
2 tablespoons finely chopped dried apricots
1 tablespoon chopped pecans
4 small slices pumpernickel bread, buttered

1 Place carrots in a medium-size bowl; drizzle honey and lemon juice over; toss to mix well. Chill at least 30 minutes to season.
2 When ready to serve, beat cream with sugar just until it mounds softly in a small bowl; fold in apricots and pecans.
3 Spoon carrot mixture on top of buttered bread slices; top with a fluff of apricot cream and a pecan half, if you wish.

Double Salad Jumbo

Zippy seasoned asparagus and carrots and crunchy chicken salad perch on crisp golden waffles.

Makes 6 servings

2 cans (5 or 6 ounces each) boned chicken, diced
1½ cups diced celery
1 tablespoon chopped parsley
½ teaspoon seasoned salt
¼ cup mayonnaise or salad dressing
1 can (1 pound) sliced carrots, drained
1 can (about 15 ounces) asparagus spears, drained
3 tablespoons bottled thin French dressing
12 frozen waffles
   Boston lettuce
   Pretzel sticks

1 Combine chicken with celery, parsley and seasoned salt in a medium-size bowl; fold in mayonnaise or salad dressing. Chill at least 30 minutes to season and blend flavors.

2 Place carrots and asparagus in separate piles in a shallow dish; drizzle French dressing over all. Chill at least 30 minutes to season.
3 Just before serving, toast waffles, following label directions; place 2 on each of 6 serving plates; top each with several leaves of lettuce.
4 Spoon ½ cup chicken salad on one waffle on each plate; arrange carrots and asparagus in bundles on remaining waffles. Garnish each plate generously with pretzel sticks.

Monterey Fiesta Sandwich

A nutritious treat, from the sunny state of California

Makes 1 sandwich.

½ small ripe avocado
2 tablespoons finely chopped green onion
1 tablespoon dairy sour cream
½ teaspoon garlic salt
Four drops liquid red pepper seasoning
2 thin corn toaster muffins
1 tablespoon butter or margarine
2 slices Monterey jack cheese, quartered
Thinly sliced tomato

1 Mash half a small ripe avocado (½ cup).
2 Add 2 tablespoons finely chopped green onion, 1 tablespoon dairy sour cream, ¼ teaspoon garlic salt and a few drops liquid red pepper seasoning.
3 Toast 2 thin corn toaster muffins; butter bottom.
4 Cut 2 slices Monterey jack cheese into 8 equal pieces. Place 2 pieces cheese, a thin slice tomato, remaining cheese and another slice tomato on each muffin.
5 Spoon guacamole mixture over tomato; top with additional chopped green onion and diced tomato.
6 Garnish with lime wedge and parsley, if you wish. Serve with knife and fork.

Cheese Rarebit Sandwich

Sometimes known as cheese "rabbit" this is satisfying winter fare

Makes 1 sandwich.

1 cup shredded sharp Cheddar cheese (4 ounces)
2 tablespoons beer or ale

1 teaspoon flour
¼ teaspoon dry mustard
Dash Worcestershire sauce
Salt and pepper
3 ½-inch thick slices French bread, toasted
Sliced green onion

1 Combine 1 cup shredded sharp Cheddar cheese, 2 tablespoons beer or ale, 1 teaspoon flour, ¼ teaspoon dry mustard, dash Worcestershire sauce, salt and pepper in the top of a double boiler.
2 Heat over hot, not boiling, water until cheese melts.
3 Pour over three ½-inch thick slices of toasted French bread.
4 Sprinkle with sliced green onion. Garnish with cherry tomato halves and watercress, if you wish.

Hunt at the market and with your purchase—a ripe avocado—create **Monterey Fiesta Sandwich.**

Cheese Rarebit is a Welsh favorite; the change in name did nothing to hurt the flavor.

Egg Burgers

When there is time for a leisurely breakfast or brunch serve these pork and egg burgers

Makes 4 servings

 4 *English muffins*
 ¼ *cup mayonnaise or salad dressing*
 ½ *teaspoon mixed salad herbs*
 1 *can (12 ounces) pork luncheon meat*
 4 *tablespoons (½ stick) butter or margarine*
 8 *eggs*
 ¼ *cup water*
 ½ *teaspoon salt*
   Dash of pepper
 ½ *cup thinly sliced celery*
 ¼ *cup shredded Cheddar cheese*
 2 *tablespoons chopped parsley*
 10 *cherry tomatoes, halved*

1 Split muffins; toast, following label directions. Blend mayonnaise or salad dressing and salad herbs in a cup; spread on muffins; keep warm.
2 Cut luncheon meat into 16 thin slices; sauté in 2 tablespoons of the butter or margarine until lightly browned in a large frying pan; keep warm.
3 Beat eggs with water just until blended in a large bowl; stir in salt, pepper and celery.
4 Melt remaining 2 tablespoons butter or margarine in a medium-size frying pan; pour in egg mixture. Cook slowly, lifting eggs around edge as they cook to let liquid part flow underneath, just until set but still shiny-moist on top.
5 Place 2 muffin halves on each of 4 serving plates; top with meat, then scrambled eggs. Sprinkle half with shredded cheese and chopped parsley, and garnish remainder with halved cherry tomatoes. Serve hot with horn-shape corn snacks and fruit punch, if you wish.

Double Corn Toasties

Packaged flat cornmeal "muffins" are heaped with fruited cottage cheese and meat

Makes 6 servings.

 1 *cup (8 ounces) cream-style cottage cheese*
 ½ *cup mandarin-orange segments (from an 11-ounce can), drained and cut up*
 6 *small leaves Boston lettuce*
 2 *packages (6 to a package) flat cornmeal cakes, toasted and lightly buttered*
   OR: 6 English muffins, split and toasted
 1 *pound sliced cooked tongue*

1 Mix cottage cheese and orange segments in a small bowl; spoon into lettuce cups. Place on 6 of the cornmeal cakes or muffin halves on serving plates; sprinkle cheese mixture with nutmeg, if you wish.
2 Fold tongue slices; lay, overlapping, on remaining cornmeal cakes or muffins; place beside cheese-topped "sandwiches" on plates.

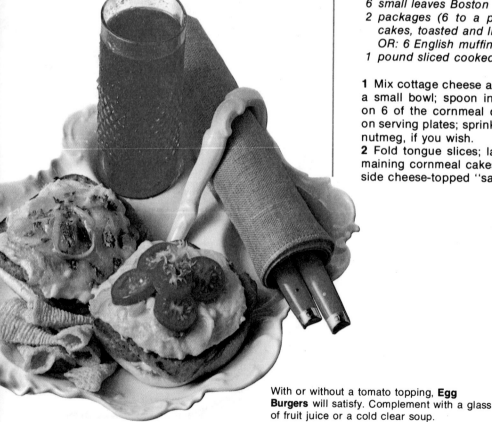

With or without a tomato topping, **Egg Burgers** will satisfy. Complement with a glass of fruit juice or a cold clear soup.

HOW TO FREEZE SANDWICHES

- *Choose a time when your kitchen is not busy and make and wrap enough sandwiches for a week or two at the most. Sandwiches start to lose their fresh flavor if frozen longer.*
- *All breads and rolls freeze well, so look for variety. As a rule of thumb, figure about 18 slices of bread in a 1-pound loaf. Again, be sure to butter bread right to the edges to prevent the filling from soaking in.*
- *Avoid fillings with watery raw vegetables—lettuce, tomato, celery, cucumber; spreads such as jelly or jam; mayonnaise or salad dressing; and hard-cooked egg whites.*
- *Dairy sour cream, milk, pineapple or orange juice, applesauce and cream cheese are all good binders for sandwich fillings to be frozen.*
- *Cut each sandwich into convenient pieces and package tightly in moisture- and vapor-proof paper or plastic sandwich bags; label, date and freeze.*
- *Pack sandwiches into the lunch box directly from the freezer. They will be thawed and fresh-tasting by lunchtime.*

Blue Cheese Open-Face Sandwiches

Top this spread with almost any favorite garnish

Makes 10 servings.

1 cup crumbled blue cheese (4 ounces)
1 cup butter, softened
10 slices rye bread
  Garnishes (see below)

Blend blue cheese and butter together in a medium-size bowl until fluffy. Spread over slices of bread. Decorate each sandwich in any of these ways:
- Top with apple wedges dipped in lemon juice.
- Top with sieved egg yolk and red caviar.
- Top with three hard-cooked egg wedges.
- Top with three cooked, shelled, deveined shrimp.
Chill all prepared sandwiches at least 30 minutes.

DELICATE PARTY SANDWICHES

Date-Nut Orange Rounds

Use the cheese-orange spread for dessert, too

Makes 30 sandwiches.

1 loaf (16 ounces) date-nut bread
8 ounces cream cheese, softened
2 tablespoons grated orange rind

1 Using a round cookie or hors d'oeuvres cutter, cut 2 rounds from each slice of bread.
2 Combine softened cream cheese and 1 tablespoon of the orange rind. Spread on bread.
3 Decorate edge of each with remaining rind.

Cream Cheese Mimosa Tea Sandwiches

Make these ahead of time and store in the refrigerator

Makes 24 sandwiches.

12 square slices dark pumpernickel bread
 8 ounces cream cheese, softened
 6 hard-cooked egg yolks, sieved
24 pimiento-stuffed green olive slices

1 Using an oval-shaped cookie or sandwich cutter (2 inches long), cut 2 ovals from each slice of bread.
2 Spread each slice with the softened cream cheese; sprinkle tops with sieved egg yolk. Top each with an olive slice.

Deviled Ham Open-Face Sandwiches

You can put these hors d'oeuvres together in a jiffy

Makes about 32 sandwiches.

16 slices white bread (about 1 pound loaf)
 2 cans (2¼ ounces each) deviled ham
 3 ounces cream cheese, softened
  Cucumber slices
  Pimiento cut-outs   *(continued)*

1 Trim crusts from bread slices; cut hearts or other decorative shapes from the slices, using 2-inch cookie or hors d'oeuvres cutters.
2 Combine ham and cream cheese until well blended; spread on bread cut-outs. Decorate with cucumber and pimiento.

Mushroom-Butter Rounds

Party nibbles with exquisite flavor

Makes 32 small sandwiches

¾ cup (1½ sticks) butter or margarine
¾ cup chopped watercress
¼ teaspoon salt
16 slices cracked-wheat bread (about 1 one-pound loaf)
8 medium-size mushrooms, sliced lengthwise
2 tablespoons lemon juice
1 can or jar (4 ounces) whole pimientos, drained

1 Blend butter or margarine, watercress, and salt in a small bowl.
2 Cut 2 rounds from each slice of bread with a 1½-inch cutter to make 32 in all; spread with watercress butter. Brush mushroom slices with lemon juice to keep them white; place one on each buttered bread round.
3 Slit pimientos down side and open out flat, then cut out tiny leaf shapes with a truffle cutter; place 2 around mushroom stems on bread rounds.
Hostess Note: Watercress butter may be spread on bread at least an hour ahead. Place sandwiches in a single layer on a cookie sheet or tray, cover tightly to prevent drying, and chill. Cut pimiento leaves ahead and chill, ready to place on sandwiches at serving time. Slice mushrooms just before serving, as they tend to darken on standing.

Ribbon Sandwich Cake

Help your party sandwich menu with these more-than-a-bite but not-too heavy sandwiches

Makes 16 servings

1 round loaf unsliced white bread
2 tablespoons butter or margarine
2 cans (about 5 ounces each) chicken spread
1 can or jar (4 ounces) pimientos, drained and chopped

1 small firm ripe avocado
1 teaspoon lemon juice
2 packages (8 ounces each) cream cheese
2 tablespoons mayonnaise or salad dressing
2 tablespoons milk
½ cup chopped parsley

1 Cut a thin slice from bread to make top flat; set aside to use for croutons or a crumb topper. Slice bottom section crosswise into 4 even layers; spread 3 of the layers with butter or margarine.
2 Mix chicken spread and pimientos in a small bowl; spread evenly on 2 of the layers.
3 Halve avocado; pit, peel and cut into small chunks; place in a small bowl. Sprinkle with lemon juice, then mash with a fork. Blend in 1 package of the cream cheese and mayonnaise or salad dressing; spread on one of the remaining layers.
4 Stack the 3 layers, with avocado layer between, on a large serving plate; place plain layer on top.
5 Beat remaining package of cream cheese with milk until fluffy-smooth in a small bowl; spread over side and top of loaf. Press parsley firmly onto side. Chill. Just before serving, garnish with a cluster of radish roses, if you wish. Cut into wedges with a sharp knife.
Hostess Note: Loaf may be made and frosted three to four hours ahead. It slices best if thoroughly chilled first.

Buffet Chicken-Sandwich Basket

It will be the talk of your party! Homemade bread is sliced and made into sandwiches, then arranged in the shell of the loaf

Bake at 350° for 50 minutes.
Makes 48 small sandwiches.

½ cup milk
3 tablespoons sugar
1½ teaspoons salt
½ cup (1 stick) butter or margarine
2 envelopes active dry yeast
½ cup very warm water
2 eggs, well beaten
4 cups sifted all-purpose flour
Sesame seeds
PARTY CHICKEN SALAD (recipe follows)

1 Scald milk with sugar, salt and butter or margarine in a small saucepan; cool to lukewarm.
2 Sprinkle yeast into very warm water in a large

There's no question but you've given your guests a good selection, when you set out **Buffet Chicken-Sandwich Basket** (left), **Lobster Top Hats** and **Ribbon Rosies** (top) and **Date-Nut Triangles** and **Pimiento-Cress Whirligigs** (bottom).

bowl. ("Very warm" water should feel comfortably warm when dropped on wrist.) Stir until yeast dissolves, then stir in cooled milk mixture and beaten eggs.

3 Beat in 2 cups of the flour until smooth. Stir in remaining flour until well blended, then beat vigorously with a spoon, scraping down side of bowl often, 100 strokes, or until dough is shiny-elastic.

4 Coat top lightly with soft butter or margarine. Cover with a clean towel; let rise in a warm place, away from draft, 1 hour, or until double in bulk.

5 Stir dough down; let rise again 30 minutes, or until double in bulk. Stir dough down again; beat another 100 strokes.

6 Grease an 8-inch spring-form pan; sprinkle bottom and side with sesame seeds; spoon dough into pan; sprinkle with sesame seeds. Cover; let rise again, 30 minutes, or until *not quite* double in bulk.

7 Bake in moderate oven (350°) 50 minutes,

(continued)

or until bread gives a hollow sound when tapped. Remove from pan; cool completely on a wire rack. Wrap and store. (Bread slices best if made a day ahead.)

8 When ready to make sandwiches, cut a thick slice from top and bottom of loaf with a sharp, long-blade knife and set aside for Steps 10 and 11. Using an up-and-down sawing motion, cut around inside crust to loosen bread in one large round; lift off shell and set aside for Step 10.

9 Slice bread into 8 thin rounds, keeping slices in order. Put each two rounds together with PARTY CHICKEN SALAD; cut each round, spoke fashion, into 12 triangular sandwiches.

10 Place bottom crust and shell of loaf from Step 8 on a large serving plate; arrange the three large rounds of sandwiches in shell. Place remaining sandwiches around edge. Cover all with a damp towel; chill.

11 When ready to serve, set top of loaf in place. Garnish with sprigs of parsley and pitted ripe olives rolled inside carrot curls and threaded onto wooden picks, if you wish. (To make carrot curls, shave a large scraped carrot into long thin strips with a vegetable parer. Roll strips around finger; hold in place with a wooden pick; chill in ice and water until curled.)

Lobster Top Hats

Tiny cherry tomato cups heaped with seafood salad perch atop cucumber sandwiches

Makes 3 dozen small sandwiches

- *1 can (about 6 ounces) lobster meat, drained, boned and finely chopped*
- *¼ cup mayonnaise or salad dressing*
- *1 tablespoon chili sauce*
- *2 small cucumbers, pared*
- *9 thin slices square rye bread*
- *9 thin slices square pumpernickel bread*
- *6 tablespoons (¾ stick) butter or margarine*
- *18 cherry tomatoes*

1 Mix lobster, mayonnaise or salad dressing and chili sauce in a small bowl. Cut each cucumber into 36 thin slices.

2 Cut 4 rounds from each slice of rye and pumpernickel bread with a 1½-inch cookie cutter; spread each with butter or margarine, then top with a cucumber slice. Stack one each rye and pumpernickel rounds, cucumber side up, to make a double-layer sandwich; repeat with remaining rounds; place on a tray. Cover with a damp towel; chill.

3 Stem tomatoes, then halve crosswise; scoop out pulp with the quarter teaspoon of a measuring-spoon set. Fill each half with lobster mixture; place in a single layer on a tray or large plate; cover; chill.

4 When ready to serve, stand a tomato-lobster cup on each cucumber sandwich, holding in place with a wooden pick, if needed. Garnish with parsley, if you wish. Arrange on serving tray.

Ribbon Rosies

How colorful they look with layers of white and whole-wheat breads striped with ham and cheese fillings

Makes 36 small sandwiches.

- *6 thin slices white bread*
- *6 thin slices whole-wheat bread*
- *6 tablespoons (¾ stick) butter or margarine*
- DEVILED HAM FILLING *(recipe follows)*
- PARSLEY-CHEESE FILLING *(recipe follows)*

1 Arrange bread in 3 rows of 4 slices each on a large cutting board, making first and third rows white and second and fourth rows whole wheat. Spread all with butter or margarine.

2 Spread DEVILED HAM FILLING on first and third rows and PARSLEY-CHEESE FILLING on second row; leave fourth row plain.

3 Place each plain slice, buttered side down, on ham-spread slice, then stack on cheese-spread slice, then on another ham-spread slice to make three 4-layer sandwiches. Wrap each in wax paper, foil or transparent wrap; chill at least 2 hours, or overnight.

4 When ready to serve, trim crusts from sandwiches. (Use trimmings for nibbles.) Cut each sandwich into quarters, then cut each quarter into 3 thin slices. Arrange on serving tray.

DEVILED HAM FILLING —Mix 1 can (4½ ounces) deviled ham, ¼ cup finely chopped celery, 2 tablespoons mayonnaise or salad dressing and 2 teaspoons prepared mustard in a small bowl. Makes ¾ cup.

PARSLEY-CHEESE FILLING —Combine ¼ cup blue-cheese spread (from a 5-ounce jar), ¼ cup finely chopped radishes and ¼ cup finely chopped parsley in a small bowl. Makes about ⅓ cup.

Date-Nut Triangles

With a simple cutting trick, canned date bread filled with fluffy orange "cream" takes on a fancy shape

Makes 40 small sandwiches

1 package (3 or 4 ounces) cream cheese
1 teaspoon grated orange peel
2 teaspoons orange juice
1 can (8 ounces) date-nut roll

1 Blend cream cheese and orange peel and juice until soft enough to spread in a small bowl.
2 Halve date-nut roll lengthwise; spread one side with half of the cheese mixture; put back together to form a roll. Halve again at right angles to first cut; spread with remaining cheese mixture; put back together. (Roll will be divided into 4 sections separated by the cheese mixture.)
3 Wrap tightly in wax paper, foil or transparent wrap. Chill at least 2 hours, or overnight.
4 When ready to serve, slice roll crosswise into 10 rounds. Lay each flat and cut into quarters, cutting through bread—not filling. Arrange on serving tray.

Pimiento-Cress Whirligigs

Recipe tells how to turn regular sliced white bread into these double-filled fancies

Makes 30 small sandwiches

½ cup (1 stick) butter or margarine
¼ cup chopped watercress leaves
1 jar (5 ounces) pimiento-cheese spread
   Few drops liquid red pepper seasoning
12 slices soft white bread

1 Cream butter or margarine in a small bowl; stir in watercress. Blend cheese spread and liquid red pepper seasoning in a second small bowl.
2 Trim crusts from bread. Line up 2 slices, slightly overlapping, on a bread board; roll thin with a rolling pin. (Slices will stick together to make a rectangle.) Spread with ⅓ of the watercress butter.
3 Roll 2 more slices of bread; spread with ⅓ of the cheese spread. Place cheese-topped slice on watercress-topped slice, leaving about ½ inch uncovered on one end; starting here, roll up, jelly-roll fashion. (This makes a neatly shaped pinwheel.)
4 Repeat with remaining bread and fillings to make 2 more rolls. Wrap each tightly in wax paper, foil or transparent wrap. Chill at least 2 hours, or overnight.
5 When ready to serve, unwrap rolls; slice each crosswise into 10 pinwheels.

HOW TO CUT SANDWICH ROLLS

A long thread makes a nifty slicer for pinwheel sandwiches and helps to keep the soft dough in trim rounds. Just place the thread around the roll, crisscross the two ends over top, and pull gently but tightly.

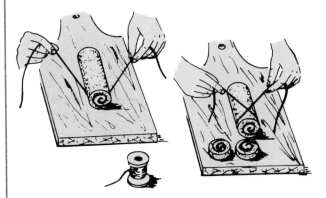

Jelly Roll-Ups

Anyone with a sweet tooth will love these miniatures

Makes 24 small sandwiches.

12 thin slices soft white bread
 6 tablespoons softened butter or margarine
½ cup currant or raspberry jelly

1 Spread bread smoothly with butter or margarine, then with jelly; cut off crusts; roll up.
2 Place, cut side down and close together, in shallow pan lined with wax paper; cover with foil, or with wax paper and a damp clean towel; chill.
3 To serve, cut each roll in half; arrange on tray.

Hostess Note: Count on about 18 slices to a 1-pound loaf of thin-sliced bread. Be sure it is fresh and soft so rolls won't crack. For 12, make half this recipe; for serving 100, buy 3 loaves and 1 pound of butter or margarine.

PARTY SANDWICH PERK-UPS

Removing delicate tart shells from muffin cups without breaking is easy if you first line cups with foil. Smooth foil as well as you can so it will peel off neatly.

For sandwich-making magic, start with bread of contrasting colors and mark each slice in triangles. Cut the same design in each, lift out with knife tip; switch trims.

Flower holder helps perky vegetable posies keep their heads high. To fix them, cut blossoms from thin carrot and green pepper slices; fasten onto slender stalks of celery with short wooden picks.

Party Chicken Salad

Diced tongue and chopped celery add colorful flecks of red and green

Makes 3 cups

    1 broiler-fryer (about 2 pounds)
    1 small onion, sliced
      Few celery tops
 1½ teaspoons salt
    ⅛ teaspoon pepper
    2 cups water
    1 can (6 ounces) tongue, finely diced (1 cup)
    1 cup chopped celery
    1 cup mayonnaise or salad dressing

1 Simmer chicken, covered, with onion, celery tops, 1 teaspoon of the salt, pepper and water in a large saucepan 45 minutes, or until chicken is tender. (Remaining salt is for salad in Step 3.)
2 Remove chicken from broth; cool until easy to handle. (Chill broth to use for soup another day.) Pull skin from chicken and take meat from bones; dice meat fine.
3 Combine with tongue, celery, mayonnaise or salad dressing and remaining ½ teaspoon salt in a medium-size bowl; toss to mix well. Chill.

Cherry-Nut Fingers

For neat slicing, bake the bread the day before, wrap and store

Bake at 350° for 1 hour.
Makes 54 sandwiches.

 2¼ cups sifted all-purpose flour
    ¾ cup sugar
    2 teaspoons baking powder
    ¾ teaspoon salt
    ½ teaspoon baking soda
    ¾ cup chopped maraschino cherries, well drained
    ½ cup chopped walnuts
    1 egg
    1 tablespoon grated orange peel
    ½ cup orange juice
    ½ cup milk
    3 tablespoons melted vegetable shortening
    1 container (8 ounces) whipped cream cheese

1 Sift flour, sugar, baking powder, salt and soda into a large bowl; stir in cherries and walnuts.
2 Beat egg in a small bowl; stir in orange peel and juice and milk; add all at once to flour mixture; add melted shortening. Stir just until

evenly moistened. Spoon into a well-greased loaf pan, 9x5x3.

3 Bake in moderate oven (350°) 1 hour, or until a wooden pick inserted in center comes out clean. Cool in pan on a wire rack 10 minutes; loosen around edges with a knife; turn out onto rack; cool completely. Wrap loaf in wax paper, foil, or transparent wrap and store overnight for easy slicing.

4 When ready to make sandwiches, trim a thin slice from each end of loaf and set aside for family nibbles. Slice remaining bread ¼ inch thick with a sharp knife. Spread half of the slices with whipped cream cheese, using 1 tablespoon for each; put together with remaining plain slices to make sandwiches. Cut each sandwich crosswise into 4 even strips. Wrap and chill until serving time.

Pumpernickel-Cream Cheese Alternates

Dark and white bread are used to assemble these

Makes 20 tea sandwiches.

10 square slices dark pumpernickel bread
5 slices white sandwich bread
1 pound (16 ounces) cream cheese, softened
1 cup finely chopped parsley

1 Trim crusts from bread slices. Combine softened cheese and parsley until well blended. Spread cheese mixture over bread slices.
2 Assemble sandwiches: Place a slice of white bread between 2 slices of pumpernickel bread. Carefully cut assembled sandwiches into quarters.

Strawberry Pinwheels

Use fresh unsliced bread for these tea sandwiches

Makes 72 to 84 pinwheels.

1 pound (16 ounces) cream cheese
2 cups strawberries, washed, hulled and sliced
2 tablespoons 10X (confectioners' powdered) sugar
1 loaf unsliced white bread

1 Soften cream cheese in medium-size bowl; blend in strawberries and sugar until smooth.

2 Cut crusts from loaf of bread, then slice bread lengthwise into 9 or 10 thin slices; cover with a dampened towel; let stand 10 minutes.
3 Spread slices, 1 at a time, with cheese mixture, using 3 to 4 tablespoonfuls per slice; roll up, jelly-roll fashion; wrap tightly in wax paper; chill.
4 Unwrap and slice rolls crosswise into pinwheels.

Deviled Ham Leaves

The decorator touch will be appreciated by guests

Makes 32 small sandwiches

32 slices soft white bread (about 2 one-pound loaves)
2 cans (4½ ounces each) deviled ham
3 cartons (4 ounces each) whipped cream cheese
Green food coloring

1 Cut two leaf shapes from each slice of bread with a 1½-inch-long cookie cutter.
2 Blend deviled ham and 2 cartons of the cream cheese until smooth in a medium-size bowl; spread on bread cutouts to make 32 sandwiches.
3 Blend remaining carton of cream cheese with a few drops food coloring to tint pale green in a small bowl.
4 Fit a plain tip onto a cake-decorating set; fill with cheese mixture. Press out onto tops of sandwiches to resemble markings on leaves.

Hostess Note: Sandwiches may be made up and decorated about an hour ahead. Place in a single layer on a cookie sheet or tray, cover tightly to keep them from drying out, and chill until serving time.

Asparagus Rolls

Tucked inside each cheese sandwich is a bright asparagus spear

Makes about 48 small sandwiches.

2 bunches fresh asparagus (about 4 pounds)
Bottled thin French dressing
3 jars (5 ounces each) sharp Cheddar cheese spread
6 tablespoons (¾ stick) butter or margarine
48 slices soft white bread (from 3 loaves)

(continued)

One of the big secrets to successful party-giving is to keep it simple—but to have a variety of eatables. And with these simple-looking but delectable **Ham Pinwheels** and **Asparagus Rolls,** and **Cherry-Nut Fingers,** you've done it all.

1 Break tough woody ends from asparagus; wash stalks well. If scales are large or sandy, cut off with a sharp knife, then wash stalks again. Cut off flowery tip of each stalk to a 3-inch length to use for sandwiches, then chill remaining to cook for a family meal.
2 Tie stalks in two or three bundles; stand upright in a deep large saucepan. Pour in boiling water to depth of about an inch; cover.
3 Cook 15 minutes, or just until crisply tender. Lift out bundles; drain; snip off strings. Place asparagus in a large shallow dish; brush with French dressing; chill several hours to season.
4 Combine cheese spread and butter or margarine in a medium-size bowl; beat until smooth.
5 Trim crusts from bread; roll each slice thin with a rolling pin; spread with cheese mixture. Place a seasoned asparagus spear at one end of each slice; roll up tightly, jelly-roll fashion. Wrap and chill.
Hostess Note: If you prefer to use frozen asparagus spears, you will need about three packages (10 ounces each). Cook and drain, following label directions, then season, following Step 3 above.

Ham Pinwheels

Peppy parsley-flecked meat filling twirls inside dainty quick-fix rolls

Bake at 375° for 15 minutes.
Makes 60 pinwheels.

2 cans (4½ ounces each) deviled ham
1 can (3 or 4 ounces) chopped mushrooms, drained and minced
¼ cup minced dill pickle
2 tablespoons chopped parsley
1 tablespoon prepared mustard
2 packages refrigerated crescent dinner rolls

1 Blend deviled ham, mushrooms, dill pickle, parsley and mustard in a small bowl.
2 Separate 1 package of the rolls into 4 rectangles; pinch dough at markings to seal. Spread each rectangle with 3 tablespoons of the ham mixture; starting at short end, roll up; pinch dough again to seal. Cut each roll into 8 even slices. Place on a large cookie sheet. Repeat with remaining package of rolls and ham filling.
3 Bake in moderate oven (375°) 15 minutes, or until golden. Serve hot or cold.

Date Fan-Tans

So easy to make—and perfect for any large-size party

Makes 56 sandwiches.

1 package (3 to 4 ounces) cream cheese
1 tablespoon milk
1 teaspoon grated orange rind
2 cans (8 ounces each) date-nut loaf

1 Blend cream cheese with milk and orange rind until spreadable.
2 Cut each date-nut loaf in half lengthwise; spread with cheese mixture; put together. Repeat lengthwise, cut at right angles; spread; put together in shape of loaf; wrap in waxed paper or foil; chill.
3 To serve, cut each loaf crosswise into ½-inch thick slices; lay on board; cut each slice into quarters through bread (not filling).
Hostess Note: A perfect make-ahead sandwich to slice just before serving. For 12, buy 1 can of date-nut loaf; for 100, 8 cans and 1 pound of cream cheese.

HOW TO ROLL PARTY BREAD

To roll bread without cracking, follow these how-tos: trim the crusts from fresh soft bread and flatten each slice. Work with only a few slices at a time to prevent the bread from drying out.

Watercress Whirls

Place salt within easy reach—many guests will enjoy the extra flavor

Makes 24 small sandwiches.

12 thin slices soft white bread
 6 tablespoons softened butter or margarine
 1 bunch watercress

1 Spread bread smoothly with butter or margarine; cut off crusts; halve each slice diagonally; roll up.
2 Place, rolled side down and close together, in shallow pan lined with wax paper; cover with foil, or with wax paper and a damp clean towel; chill.
3 Wash and dry watercress; snip tops into 1-inch-long sprigs; wrap loosely; chill.
4 To serve, stick a watercress sprig in open end of each roll; arrange on tray.

Hostess Note: Make half this recipe to serve 12; for 100 use three one-pound loaves of bread and 1 pound of butter or margarine.

Cherry Blossoms

These dainty pinwheels, flavored with almonds and cherries, start with unsliced bread. Be sure to order it ahead

Makes 60-70 small sandwiches.

1 package (8 ounces) cream cheese
2 tablespoons very finely chopped maraschino cherries
2 tablespoons maraschino-cherry syrup
2 tablespoons very finely chopped toasted slivered almonds (from a 5-ounce can)
1 cup (2 sticks) butter or margarine
1 loaf unsliced fresh white bread

1 Soften cream cheese in a medium-size bowl; blend in cherries, syrup and almonds. Soften butter or margarine until easy to spread in a small bowl.
2 Trim crusts from loaf of bread, then slice bread lengthwise into 8 thin slices. Cover with damp towel; let stand 10 minutes.
3 Spread slices, 1 at a time, with about 2 tablespoons softened butter or margarine, then about 2 tablespoons cheese mixture. Starting at end, roll up, jelly-roll style. Wrap tightly in
(continued)

wax paper, foil or transparent wrap. Chill at least 2 hours, or overnight.

4 To serve, unwrap and slice each roll crosswise into 8 or 9 slices.

Hostess Note: Use your sharpest knife, as bread must be sliced thin and even. We found it easier to cut crusts from bottom, sides and ends, leaving top to hold onto. As you slice rolls, wipe knife often so filling will not smear. For serving 100, make 2 to 3 times the recipe, depending on the varieties of other sandwiches in your tea menu:

Mint Jewels

Ladyfingers are the starter for these little sweet tea sandwiches

Makes 48 small sandwiches.

8 ladyfingers
3 tablespoons butter or margarine, softened
10 preserved kumquats, drained and sliced thin
1 tablespoon mint jelly

1 Separate ladyfingers to make 16 pieces; spread with softened butter or margarine. Cut each piece crosswise into thirds.

2 Top each with a kumquat slice, then a dot of mint jelly; place in single layer on large plate. Cover wiith wax paper, foil or transparent wrap; chill.

Hostess Note: These little treats are real tempters. They are good keepers, too, even as long as overnight, if covered and chilled. For serving 100, make 3 or 4 times the recipe.

Cucumber Towers

Cucumber slices make the crisp filling for these triple-deck sandwiches

Makes 48 small sandwiches.

1 large cucumber
18 thin slices white bread (about 1 loaf)
6 tablespoons (¾ stick) butter or margarine, softened
1 jar (about 4 ounces) tiny pickled onions, drained
1 can (4 ounces) pimientos, drained and cut into tiny squares or circles

1 Score rind of cucumber with a fork, then cut cucumber into 24 thin slices.

2 Cut 2 rounds from each slice of bread with a 2-inch cutter; spread rounds with butter or margarine, using about a half teaspoonful for each.

3 Make 12 sandwiches, each with 2 slices of cucumber between 3 rounds of bread. Place on tray lined with a damp towel; cover; chill.

4 Thread 2 pickled onions and 2 pieces of pimiento onto sharp end of a wooden pick for each kebab; place on a plate; cover with wax paper, foil or transparent wrap; chill.

5 When ready to serve, place 4 kebabs in each sandwich round, sticking pick to bottom to hold round together. Cut rounds into quarters with sharp knife.

Hostess Note: These sandwiches are perfect make-aheads if tray is covered and kept chilled. For serving 100, make 3 times the recipe.

Strawberry Cornucopias

Fruit-filled jewels that will disappear fast

Makes 32 small sandwiches

3 cups (1½ pints) strawberries
1 package (8 ounces) cream cheese
2 tablespoons 10X (confectioners' powdered) sugar
¼ cup finely chopped walnuts
32 slices soft white bread (about two 1-pound loaves)

1 Wash strawberries and hull; mash enough to measure 2 tablespoonfuls in a medium-size bowl; set remainder aside.

2 Beat cream cheese and 10X sugar into mashed strawberries until smooth; stir in walnuts.

3 Cut a round from center of each slice of bread with a 3-inch cookie cutter; roll each thin with a rolling pin. Spread a rounded teaspoonful cream-cheese mixture over each; roll into a cornucopia shape.

4 Halve remaining strawberries; tuck one half into end of each sandwich.

Hostess Note: Sandwiches may be made up about an hour ahead. Place in a single layer on a cookie sheet or tray, cover tightly to prevent drying and chill. Add strawberry garnish just before serving so color doesn't run.

HOW TO STORE PARTY SANDWICHES

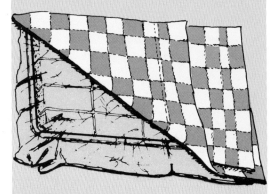

Depend on your refrigerator to hold make-ahead dainties appetizingly fresh and moist until serving time. Place them in a shallow pan lined with damp paper toweling and transparent wrap; cover and keep chilled.

Harlequins

A hostess' joy of a sandwich, for many can be made in a short time

Makes 48 sandwiches.

8 thin slices whole-wheat bread (about ½ loaf)
8 thin slices white bread (about ½ loaf)
½ cup (1 stick) butter or margarine, softened
    PARSLEY-CREAM-CHEESE FILLING *(recipe follows)*
    EGG FILLING *(recipe follows)*

1 Arrange bread in 4 rows of 4 slices each on large cutting board, making first and fourth rows whole wheat, second and third rows white; spread all with softened butter or margarine.
2 Spread PARSLEY-CREAM-CHEESE FILLING on first (whole wheat) and third (white) rows; spread EGG FILLING on second (white) row.
3 Place each fourth-row (whole wheat) slice, buttered side down, on parsley-cream-cheese slice; then stack on egg-spread slice, then on parsley-cream-cheese slice to make 4 four-decker sandwiches; cut off crusts; wrap each in waxed paper, transparent saran, or foil; chill.
4 To serve, cut each into quarters, then cut each quarter into 3 thin slices.

PARSLEY-CREAM-CHEESE FILLING
Soften 1 package (8 ounces) cream cheese in medium-size bowl; blend in 2 tablespoons milk (to make cheese smoothly spreadable) and 1½ cups finely chopped parsley. Makes about 1 cup.

EGG FILLING
Chop 3 hard-cooked eggs finely; combine in small bowl with 3 tablespoons mayonnaise, 1 teaspoon prepared mustard, and ¼ teaspoon salt. Makes about ½ cup.

Hostess Note: These sandwiches are wonderful make-aheads; in fact, they can be prepared a whole day ahead, wrapped in waxed paper or transparent saran and a dampened towel, or in foil, and kept chilled. Just before serving, do the final cutting *(Step 4 above)*. For 100, make 4 times the fillings and buy 2 loaves each of thin-sliced white and whole-wheat breads and 1 pound butter or margarine.

Cheese Swirls

They look just as good arranged on the party table as they are to snack on

Makes 48 to 60 sandwiches.

1 loaf (1 pound) unsliced soft white bread
¼ cup (½ stick) butter or margarine, softened
1 container (6 ounces) Cheddar-flavor cold-pack cheese food

1 Cut unsliced soft white bread lengthwise into 5 or 6 slices; trim crusts.
2 Spread to edges with softened butter or margarine, then with Cheddar-flavor cheese spread (from a 6-ounce container).
3 Roll up, jelly-roll fashion; wrap; label, date, and freeze. To serve, cut each roll crosswise into about 8 to 12 slices.

Salad Cones

The hostess with the mostest will have plenty of these on hand

Makes 24 cones.

1 loaf (1½ pounds) thin-sliced soft white bread
½ cup (1 stick) butter or margarine, softened
    CHICKEN SALAD *(recipe follows)*

1 Trim crusts from thin-sliced soft white bread; flatten each slice with rolling pin;

(continued)

spread to edges with softened butter or margarine.

2 Spoon 1½ tablespoons CHICKEN SALAD in center; fold bread diagonally; press edges to form cones.

3 Arrange in single layer on a foil-lined tray.

CHICKEN SALAD

Mix 2 cups minced cooked chicken, ½ cup minced toasted almonds, 2 tablespoons minced parsley, 4 teaspoons lemon juice, ½ teaspoon salt, ½ teaspoon curry powder, and 1 cup dairy sour cream in bowl. Makes about 2½ cups.

Ribbon Squares

Partytime can be hurry-up time—these quick-to-do sandwiches help smooth out the party preparation time

Makes 16 sandwiches.

6 slices white bread
6 slices whole wheat bread
¼ cup (½ stick) butter or margarine, softened
1 container (5 ounces) pineapple-cheese spread

1 Spread 6 slices each white and whole-wheat bread with softened butter or margarine.

2 Spread all but 2 slices of each with pineapple-cheese spread (from a 5-ounce jar).

3 Make 3-decker sandwiches, alternating dark and light slices.

4 To serve, remove crusts; cut each sandwich into quarters.

Parsley Logs

Colorful snacks that look good on the buffet table

Makes 24 sandwiches.

12 slices thin-sliced soft white bread
⅓ cup butter or margarine, softened
3 tablespoons finely chopped parsley

1 Trim crusts from 12 slices thin-sliced soft white bread; flatten each slice with rolling pin.

2 Spread slices to edges with mixture of 6 tablespoons softened butter or margarine and 3 tablespoons finely chopped parsley; roll.

3 To serve, cut each roll in half diagonally.

Beehive Buffet Sandwich

Perfect for a buffet—cut the sandwich bread then add two fillings

Makes 40 sandwiches.

1 round loaf (1 pound) rye bread
CUCUMBER CHEESE (recipe follows)
BUTTER CRESS (recipe follows)

1 Slice top crust from a round 1-pound loaf rye bread, forming a lid; halve loaf, top to bottom. With cut side down, slice 1 half lengthwise into 10 thin slices; repeat with second half, keeping all slices in order for restacking.

2 Make CUCUMBER-CHEESE sandwiches with half the sliced loaf, BUTTER-CRESS sandwiches with other half.

3 Restack sandwiches to re-form loaf; top with cut-off crust; wrap in foil or plastic food wrap; chill several hours or overnight.

4 Before serving, remove crust lid and carefully cut each half into quarters to make thin wedge-shape sandwiches; cut a slit in lid.

5 Make a "bouquet" of carrot sticks, radishes, and parsley; insert in slit and place atop loaf.

CUCUMBER-CHEESE

Blend 1 package (8 ounces) cream cheese, ½ cup finely chopped pared cucumber (no seeds), ¼ cup sour cream, 1 teaspoon cut chives, and salt and pepper to taste in small bowl. Makes about 1½ cups.

BUTTER-CRESS

Spread bread to edges with whipped butter (from an 8-ounce carton); cover with a layer of cleaned dry water-cress leaves (no stems).

SANDWICH FILLINGS

Swiss-Ham Spread

This is an excellent make-ahead spread, for it will keep well for a week or more if covered and stored in the refrigerator

Makes about 3 cups—enough spread for 12 to 16 pancakes.

1 can (12 ounces) pork luncheon meat
½ pound Swiss cheese

¾ cup mayonnaise or salad dressing
¼ cup pickle relish
1 tablespoon prepared mustard
1 teaspoon vinegar

Break up meat with fork in bowl; grate in cheese (or put cheese through food chopper, using medium blade); blend in remaining ingredients.

Green Tomato Sandwich Spread

Whip up a batch of this spread that adds a little pizzazz to almost any kind of sandwich

Makes about 1 quart.

1 pint green tomatoes
2 red peppers
2 green peppers
2 tablespoons salt
1 cup water
6 sweet pickles, ground or finely chopped
1 cup sugar
2 tablespoons flour
3 eggs, beaten
1½ cups cider vinegar
½ cup dairy sour cream

1 Wash and stem a pint of green tomatoes. Grind and drain. (If you don't have a grinder, whirl in the blender, or chop finely.)
2 Add two each red and green peppers (or four of either color if you · prefer), seeded and ground, and 2 tablespoons salt. Let stand for 15 minutes; drain again.
3 Place vegetables in a heavy, medium-size kettle and cover with 1 cup water. Bring to a boil, lower heat and simmer gently till tender, stirring occasionally.
4 Add 6 sweet pickles, ground or finely chopped, and keep mixture hot.
5 In another medium-size saucepan, combine 1 cup sugar, 2 tablespoons flour, 3 beaten eggs, 1½ cups cider vinegar and ½ cup dairy sour cream; cook, stirring, until thick.
6 Add dressing to vegetable mixture and blend thoroughly. It will keep in your refrigerator for about a week.
NOTE: This spread also makes a tasty salad dressing—spoon some over chilled lettuce wedges for a change from tossed salad, or use it in place of your ordinary dressing on potato or macaroni salad. For a taste sensation, try mixing it with a can of tuna—its versatility is practically boundless.

SANDWICH FILLINGS THAT FREEZE WELL

• Ground roast beef, lamb, pork, ham, veal or chicken moistened with gravy and seasoned with grated onion, prepared horseradish or Worcestershire sauce.
• Chopped cooked chicken livers or calf's or lamb liver mixed with mashed hard-cooked egg yolk, minced onion and catsup.
• Cream cheese, chopped stuffed olives and salted peanuts moistened with undiluted evaporated milk.
• Mashed sardines, lemon juice and grated cheese.
• Sliced tongue and American cheese with mustard pickle.
• Sliced roast lamb on bread spread with mint-seasoned butter. (Cream 1 stick butter or margarine with 1 tablespoon chopped fresh mint.)
• Peanut butter and honey; peanut butter and crisp bacon bits; peanut butter and applesauce; peanut butter and sliced sweet pickle.
• Canned corned beef or liver spread seasoned with grated onion, chopped pickle or chili sauce.
• Sliced meat loaf, sliced Swiss cheese and mustard.
• Chopped hard-cooked egg yolks, crisp bacon bits, grated onion and catsup.
• Deviled ham, chopped mustard pickle relish, and mashed hard-cooked egg yolks.
• Ground cooked ham, ground Cheddar cheese, minced onion and chili sauce.
• Canned tuna on bread spread with savory butter. (Cream 1 stick butter or margarine with 2 tablespoons catsup, mustard-pickle relish or tomato-pickle relish.)
• Chopped cooked chicken, chopped salted almonds and cream cheese softened with milk.
• Thinly sliced frankfurters with baked beans and mustard-pickle relish.
• Chili con carne and chopped onion.
• Cream cheese and blue cheese (equal parts) moistened with milk.

For an impressive and exciting buffet table, set out a full-service sandwich bar—with meats—salami, ham slices, beef, poultry—cheeses, and vegetables, and different types of breads.

QUICK AND EASY FILLINGS

- Chop corned beef finely; moisten with chili sauce and a bit of prepared horse-radish.
- Chop hard-cooked eggs, crisp bacon, and pimiento; blend in dairy sour cream for richness and a little curry powder for punch.
- Mix peanut butter, crunchy or cream-style, with grated raw carrot and finely diced celery. Stir in a little mayonnaise or bottled coleslaw dressing to make it spreadable.
- Mash liverwurst or braunschweiger; add chopped celery; season with a little dairy sour cream and prepared mustard.
- Grate equal parts Cheddar cheese and Swiss cheese (or put through food chopper); moisten with undiluted evaporated

milk; sprinkle generously with caraway seeds.
- Combine deviled ham, mustard-pickle relish, mashed hard-cooked eggs.
- Season canned corned beef or liver spread with grated onion, chopped pickle, or chili sauce.
- Blend equal parts softened butter or margarine and cream cheese; moisten with a little mayonnaise or thick salad dressing. Use plain or blend in chopped stuffed olives, minced cooked ham seasoned with mustard-pickle relish, or equal parts finely diced celery and grated raw carrot.
- Blend chopped cooked chicken, chopped salted almonds, and cream cheese softened with milk.

Liver-Cheese Pâté

An ever-popular sandwich filling

Makes about 2 cups.

½ *pound liverwurst*
1 *package (8 ounces) cream cheese*
3 *tablespoons milk*
1½ *teaspoons lemon juice*

1 Remove skin from liverwurst; mash meat with fork in medium-size bowl.
2 Blend in cream cheese, then milk and lemon juice to make a smooth paste. (An electric mixer or blender does a quick job.)

Blintz Spread

A delicious cottage cheese and strawberry jam spread for party pancakes

Makes 2 cups, enough for 12-16 pancakes.

1 *container (8 ounces) cream-style cottage cheese*
1 *cup (from a 1-pound jar) strawberry jam*
Pancakes (see index for recipe)

1 Empty 1 cup (8-ounce container) cottage cheese into a small bowl.
2 Put 1 cup (from a 1-pound jar) strawberry jam into a second bowl.
3 To use: spread each pancake with cheese, then with jam; top with a second pancake; fold in half for easy eating.

Cream Cheese and Parsley Filling

Smooth and easy to apply

Makes about ½ cup.

1 *package (3 or 4 ounces) cream cheese*
2 *tablespoons fresh parsley*

1 Soften 3- to 4-ounce package cream cheese in small bowl.
2 Stir in 2 teaspoons well dried fresh parsley, chopped.

A fast-made soup with a delicious flavor, **Oyster Chowder** starts with canned oyster stew and canned lobster. Add potatoes, whole-kernel corn, and peas (see index for recipe).

Soups To Spike the Appetite

If you've ever been tantalized by the smell of soup simmering on the stove, you'll find much to be glad of in this chapter. There are soups that are served before the meal, and soups that take the place of a main dish. Soups that are thick, others that are thin. Some which are hot, and some, cold. And for those who enjoy the richness of crockery cooking, a special section of crockery pot special soups. In short, a soup for every occasion, and every taste.

BASIC SOUP STOCKS

Basic Beef Stock

Make this flavorful beef broth that is the basic stock for a variety of soups to follow

Makes 14 cups

2½ pounds brisket, boneless chuck or bottom round, in one piece
2 pounds shin of beef with bones
2 three-inch marrow bones
1 veal knuckle (about 1 pound)
   Water
8 teaspoons salt
2 carrots, pared
2 medium-size yellow onions, peeled
2 stalks celery with leaves
1 turnip, pared and quartered
1 leek, washed well
3 large sprigs of parsley
12 peppercorns
3 whole cloves
1 bay leaf

1 Place beef, shin of beef, marrow bones and veal knuckle in a large kettle; add water to cover, about 4 quarts. Heat to boiling; skim off foam that appears on top. Add salt, carrots, onions, celery, turnip and leek; tie parsley, peppercorns, cloves and bay leaf in a small cheesecloth bag; add to kettle. Push under the liquid and add more water if needed.
2 Heat to boiling; cover; reduce heat; simmer very slowly 3½ to 4 hours, or until meat is tender. Remove meat and vegetables from broth.
3 Strain broth through cheesecloth into a large bowl. (There should be about 14 cups.) Use this stock in any recipe calling for beef broth.
4 When meat is cool enough to handle, remove and discard bones. Trim large piece of meat and save for a main-dish recipe, if you wish. Cut trimmings and shin beef into bite-size pieces; use as called for in following recipes. To store in refrigerator up to 3 to 4 days, keep in covered container. To freeze, pack in small portions, 1 or 2 cups, in plastic bags or freezer containers, to use as needed.
5 To store in refrigerator, up to 4 days, leave fat layer on surface of broth until ready to use, then lift off and discard before heating. To freeze: Transfer broth to freezer containers, allowing space on top for expansion; freeze until ready to use (3 to 4 months maximum).

Basic Chicken Stock

It is well worthwhile to make homemade chicken broth. This recipe gives you enough broth and meat to make 2 soups and even extra meat for a salad or casserole, if you wish

Makes 12 cups

2 broiler-fryers, 3 to 3½ pounds each
   Chicken giblets
2 medium carrots, pared
1 large parsnip, pared
1 large onion, chopped (1 cup)
2 stalks celery
2 celery tops
3 sprigs parsley
1 leek, washed well
   Water
2 tablespoons salt
12 peppercorns

1 Combine chicken, chicken giblets, carrots, parsnip, onion and celery in a large kettle; tie celery tops, parsley and leek together with a string; add to kettle. Add enough cold water to cover chicken and vegetables, about 12 cups.
2 Heat slowly to boiling; skim; add salt and peppercorns; reduce heat. Simmer very slowly 1 to 1½ hours, or until meat falls off the bones. Remove meat and vegetables, discard the bundle of greens.

(continued)

3 Strain broth through cheesecloth into a large bowl. (There should be about 12 cups.) Use this delicious stock in any recipe calling for chicken broth.

4 When cool enough to handle, remove and discard skin and bones from chicken; cut meat into bite-size pieces; use as called for in following recipes, or use in salads, casseroles, etc. To store in refrigerator, up to 3 to 4 days, keep in covered container. To freeze, pack in small portions, 1 or 2 cups, in plastic bags or freezer containers, to use as needed.

5 To store in refrigerator, up to 4 days, leave fat layer on surface of broth until ready to use, then lift fat off and discard, or use in other cooking. To freeze, transfer broth to freezer containers, allowing space on top for expansion. Freeze until ready to use (3 to 4 months maximum).

Basic Vegetable Stock

The basic vegetable stock for many recipes that follow

Makes about 6 cups

    4 cups water
    2 cups chopped celery stalks and leaves
    1 large onion, chopped
    ½ cup chopped cabbage
    1 carrot diced
    6 peppercorns
 1½ teaspoons salt
    1 bay leaf
    ¼ teaspoon monosodium glutamate
 2½ cups (1 No. 2 can) tomato juice

Combine all ingredients in a 3-quart saucepan; simmer covered about 1 hour; strain. Serve hot as vegetable bouillon, or use as a stock for making soup.

SPECIALS FROM THE CROCKERY POT

Basic Vegetable Soup

You don't have to be a vegetarian to love this tasty broth. Excellent between meals for dieters

Cook on 190° to 200° for 6 hours,
or on 290° to 300° for 3 hours.
Makes 6 servings.

    4 cups water
    2 cups chopped celery stalks and leaves
    1 large onion, chopped (1 cup)
    ½ cup chopped cabbage
    1 carrot, diced
    6 peppercorns
 1½ teaspoons salt
    1 bay leaf
    ¼ teaspoon monosodium glutamate
 2½ cups tomato juice

1 Combine water, celery, onion, cabbage, carrot, peppercorns, salt, bay leaf and monosodium glutamate in slow cooker; cover.
2 Cook on low (190° to 200°) 6 hours, or on high (290° to 300°) 3 hours; strain. Serve as vegetable bouillon, or as a base for making other soups.

Mulligatawny Soup

A classic soup with origins in India—is richly flavored with exotic curry

Cook on 190° to 200° for 4 hours,
or on 290° to 300° for 2 hours.
Makes 6 servings.

    1 large onion, chopped (1 cup)
    ¼ cup (½ stick) butter or margarine
    1 medium-size apple, pared, quartered, cored
        and chopped
    5 teaspoons curry powder
    1 teaspoon salt
    ¼ cup all-purpose flour
    3 medium-size carrots, pared and sliced
    2 stalks of celery, sliced
    6 cups CLASSIC CHICKEN BROTH (recipe follows)
    3 cups cooked diced chicken
    1 tablespoon lemon juice
    2 cups hot cooked rice
    ¼ cup chopped parsley
    6 lemon slices (optional)

1 Sauté onion until soft in butter or margarine in skillet or electric slow cooker with browning unit; stir in apple, curry powder and salt; sauté 5 minutes longer, or until apple is soft; add flour.
2 Combine onion mixture, carrots, celery, CLASSIC CHICKEN BROTH and chicken in slow cooker. Cover.
3 Cook on low (190° to 200°) 4 hours, or on high (290° to 300°) 2 hours. Stir in lemon juice.
4 Ladle into soup plates or bowls; pass hot cooked rice and chopped parsley and lemon slices, if you wish, for each to add his own garnish. Good with crusty French bread.

Danish Oxtail Soup

Laugh at rainy days when you have this bubbling soup waiting at home in your slow cooker

Bake at 450° for 45 minutes.
Cook on 190° to 200° for 8 hours,
or on 290° to 300° for 4 hours.
Makes 6 servings.

3 pounds oxtails, cut up
1 large onion, chopped (1 cup)
2 large carrots, pared and sliced
1 large parsnip, pared and sliced
1 white turnip, pared and sliced
2 tablespoons brandy
6 cups water
1 tablespoon salt
½ teaspoon pepper
½ teaspoon leaf savory, crumbled
1 bay leaf
  EGGS MIMOSA *(recipe follows)*
  Chopped parsley

1 Spread oxtails in a single layer in shallow roasting pan. Roast in very hot oven (450°) for 45 minutes, or until nicely browned. Drain off fat, reserving 2 tablespoons in pan.
2 Sauté onion, carrots, parsnip and turnip in reserved fat in a large skillet or an electric slow cooker with a browning unit, 10 minutes, or until soft. Add browned oxtails. Drizzle brandy over; ignite carefully with a lighted match.
3 Place oxtail mixture in slow cooker; add water, salt, pepper, savory and bay leaf; cover slow cooker.
4 Cook on low (190° to 200°) 8 hours, or on high (290° to 300°) 4 hours, or until oxtails are tender.
5 Ladle into soup bowls; place half an EGG MIMOSA in each, sprinkle with parsley. Serve with crusty French bread.

EGGS MIMOSA
Cut 3 hard-cooked eggs in half lengthwise. Carefully remove yolks, keeping whites whole. Press yolks through a sieve; spoon back into whites.

FOOD SAFETY TEMPERATURES

The USDA has set up this chart as a guide to the safest temperatures for holding various foods:

0°	*Safest temperature to store frozen foods. Do not store foods above 10°.*
32° to 40°	*The best temperature for holding foods in refrigerator.*
60° to 125°	*DANGER ZONE for all perishable foods.*
140° to 165°	*This is the temperature at which bacteria begin to be destroyed in cooking. Foods can be warmed at 140°, but not cooked.*
212°	*This is the temperature that a water-bath canner reaches and is safe for most jams, jellies, pickles and high-acid tomatoes.*
240°	*This is the temperature at which to process all low-acid vegetables, meats and poultry in a home-size pressure canner.*

Classic Chicken Broth

You see it called for in gourmet recipes: now let your slow cooker do the work while you're away—or even asleep

Cook on 190° to 200° for 10 hours,
or on 290° to 300° for 5 hours.
Makes 12 cups.

1 stewing chicken (about 5 pounds)
2 medium-size carrots, pared
1 large white parsnip, pared
1 large onion, chopped (1 cup)
2 stalks celery with leaves, chopped
  Handful parsley
10 cups water
2 tablespoons salt
12 peppercorns

(continued)

1 Combine chicken with giblets, but not livers, in a 5-quart electric slow cooker. Add carrots, parsnip, onion, celery, and parsley; pour water over; sprinkle with salt and peppercorns; cover.
2 Cook on low (190° to 200°) 10 hours, or on high (290° to 300°) 5 hours, or until chicken is tender; remove chicken and vegetables from broth.
3 Strain broth through cheesecloth into a large bowl. (There should be about 12 cups.) Cool chicken until cool enough to handle; remove and discard skin and bones. Save chicken meat for use in casseroles or cold salads.
4 Refrigerate broth, up to 4 days, leaving the fat layer on surface until ready to use; then lift off and discard. To freeze broth, pour into re-cipe-size plastic freezer containers to within ½-inch of top; seal; label and date. Freeze. Plan to use within 3 months.

Company Soup

Garnish this tasty soup with bacon, green onions and cucumbers

Cook on 190° to 200° for 5 hours,
or on 290° to 300° for 3 hours.
Makes 6 servings.

  3 cans (13¾ ounces each) chicken broth
  ¼ cup dry white wine
1½ cups chopped cooked chicken
  1 package (10 ounces) frozen green peas, thawed
  1 can (5 ounces) water chestnuts, sliced
  ⅓ cup sliced ripe olives
1½ teaspoons salt
  ⅛ teaspoon pepper
  1 teaspoon leaf tarragon, crumbled
    Chopped cooked bacon
    Sliced green onions
    Cucumber slices

1 Combine chicken broth, wine, chicken, peas, water chestnuts, olives, salt, pepper and tar-ragon in an electric slow cooker; cover.
2 Cook on low (190° to 200°) 5 hours, or on high (290° to 300°) 3 hours.
3 Ladle into soup bowls and pass tiny bowls of bacon, green onions and cucumber to sprinkle on top.

Lima Bean Soup

An old-time favorite that still delights families

Cook on 190° to 200° for 10 hours,
or on 290° to 300° for 5 hours.
Makes 6 servings.

1 package (1 pound) dried large lima beans
5 cups water
1 meaty bone from baked ham
1 medium-size onion, diced (½ cup)
1 teaspoon salt
¼ teaspoon pepper
1 to 2 cups milk

1 Wash beans and pick over; combine with water in a kettle. Heat to boiling; cook 2 minutes; cover. Remove from heat; let stand 1 hour.
2 Combine soaked beans and liquid, ham bone, onion, salt and pepper in slow cooker; cover.
3 Cook on low (190° to 200°) 10 hours, or on high (290° to 300°) 5 hours, or until beans are tender.
4 Remove ham bone and cool until easy to handle. Strip off meat, removing any fat; dice meat; return to slow cooker.
5 Stir in 1 to 2 cups milk, depending on how thick you like soup. Turn heat control to high (290° to 300°); heat 15 minutes.
6 Ladle into soup bowls; sprinkle with chopped parsley and serve with French bread, if you wish.

English Giblet Soup

Frugal British cooks have always known how to get the most from a chicken

Cook on 190° to 200° for 10 hours,
or on 290° to 300° for 5 hours.
Makes 6 servings.

1 pound chicken giblets
3 tablespoons butter or margarine
½ cup all-purpose flour
8 cups CLASSIC CHICKEN BROTH (see index for recipe)
  OR: 8 envelopes or teaspoons instant chicken broth and 8 cups water
2 teaspoons salt
¼ teaspoon pepper
1 bay leaf
2 cups cooked rice
½ cup chopped celery

1 Sauté chicken giblets in butter or margarine in a large skillet or an electric slow cooker with a browning unit.
2 Stir in flour and cook, stirring constantly, 5 minutes, or until flour browns.
3 Combine chicken giblets with CLASSIC CHICKEN BROTH or instant chicken broth and water, salt, pepper and bay leaf in an electric slow cooker; cover.
4 Cook on low (190° to 200°) 10 hours, or on high (290° to 300°) 5 hours, or until giblets are tender.
5 Stir in rice and celery and cook 15 minutes to heat rice. Serve in heated soup bowls topped with chopped parsley, if you wish.

QUICK SOUP TIPS

● *Try slipping a strip of orange and/or lemon rind into a soup, stew or pot roast, or into a saucepan of vegetables as they cook. Rinds can add exquisite flavor at no extra expense. The easiest way to peel an orange or lemon so that you get the colored part of the rind only, not the bitter white part, is with a swivel-bladed vegetable peeler.*
● *Stir canned seafood—shrimps, crab, lobster or tuna—into canned condensed vegetable soup and seasoned stewed tomatoes for a fast gumbo.*
● *For an instant tomato bouillon, heat 2½ cups canned tomato juice and 1 can (10½ ounces) condensed beef broth with 1 teaspoon crumbled leaf basil just to boiling; serve hot with a garnish of popcorn.*

Scandinavian Supper Soup

In the land of the Midnight Sun, families appreciate steaming bowls of thick pea soup: your family will, too

Cook on 190° to 200° for 10 hours,
or on 290° to 300° for 5 hours.
Makes 8 servings.

1 package (1 pound) dried yellow split peas
6 cups boiling water
½ pound lean salt pork
3 large carrots, pared and sliced
1 large leek, trimmed and sliced
1 large onion, chopped (1 cup)
1 teaspoon salt
1 teaspoon leaf thyme, crumbled

¼ teaspoon pepper
1 pound frankfurters, scored
Chopped parsley

1 Pick over peas and rinse under running water; place peas in an electric slow cooker; pour in boiling water; cover. Let stand 1 hour.
2 Score salt pork and push down into peas; add carrots, leek, onion, salt, thyme, pepper and frankfurters; cover.
3 Cook on low (190° to 200°) 10 hours, stirring after 5 hours, if possible, or on high (290° to 300°) 5 hours, stirring after 3 hours, if possible.
4 Ladle soup into soup bowls; sprinkle with chopped parsley.

Petite Marmite Henry IV

Marmite is French for stock pot: Henry IV was the French king who promised a chicken in every pot

Cook on 190° to 200° for 10 hours,
or on 290° to 300° for 5 hours.
Makes 8 servings.

1 stewing chicken (about 5 pounds)
1 pound boneless chuck
½ pound chicken wings
1 pound beef bones
12 cups cold water
2 large carrots, pared and sliced
3 leeks, trimmed and sliced
2 stalks celery, chopped
1 white turnip, pared and diced
1 large onion stuck with 6 cloves
1 tablespoon salt
Handful parsley
2 cloves garlic, peeled
5 peppercorns
1 bay leaf

1 Place chicken, beef, chicken wings, and beef bones in a 5-quart electric slow cooker; add water, carrots, leeks, celery, turnip, onion and salt. Tie parsley, garlic, peppercorns and bay leaf in cheesecloth; add to cooker; cover.
2 Cook on low (190° to 200°) 10 hours, or on high (290° to 300°) 5 hours, or until chicken is tender. Remove chicken and beef. Let cool enough to handle, then slice or cut in julienne pieces; reserve.
3 Strain broth through cheesecloth into a heated soup tureen; add meat and freshly cooked carrot and turnip slices, if you wish. Taste and season with additional salt and pepper.

Winter's Best Soup

If this is waiting in your slow cooker you don't have to be afraid of the coldest days

Cook on 190° to 200° for 10 hours,
or on 290° to 300° for 5 hours.
Makes 6 servings.

3 three-inch beef marrow bones
1 beef knuckle bone, cracked
10 cups water
1 can (about 1 pound) tomatoes
3 medium-size carrots, pared and diced
2 small white turnips, pared and diced
1 medium-size onion, chopped (½ cup)
1 cup diced celery
6 whole cloves
1 bay leaf
1 teaspoon leaf thyme, crumbled
2 teaspoons salt
1 teaspoon sugar
¼ teaspoon pepper
1 cup dried lima beans (from a 1-pound package)
½ pound green beans, tipped and cut
1 cup shell macaroni, cooked
2 cups chopped raw spinach
MARROW BALLS (recipe follows)

1 Remove marrow from marrow bones to make MARROW BALLS.
2 Combine bones and water, tomatoes, carrots, turnips, onion, celery, cloves, bay leaf, thyme, salt, sugar, pepper, lima beans and green beans in slow cooker; cover.
3 Cook on low (190° to 200°) 10 hours, or on high (290° to 300°) 5 hours.
4 Remove bones, bay leaf and whole cloves; skim off fat; add macaroni, turn heat control to high (290° to 300°); add spinach and MARROW BALLS; cover; cook 15 minutes.

Marrow Balls

½ cup mashed beef marrow (from beef marrow bones)
1 cup soft bread crumbs
1 egg, beaten
1 tablespoon minced parsley
½ teaspoon salt
⅛ teaspoon pepper

1 Combine mashed beef marrow, bread crumbs, egg, parsley, salt and pepper in small bowl.
2 Form lightly into 24 balls.

Hungarian Goulash Soup

Hungary is the only country that grows paprika—in this world

Cook on 190° to 200° for 8 hours,
or on 290° to 300° for 4 hours.
Makes 8 servings.

2 tablespoons vegetable shortening
1½ pounds lean beef, cubed
1 tablespoon paprika
¼ cup tomato purée
6 cups CLASSIC BEEF BROTH (see index for recipe)
   OR: 6 envelopes or teaspoons instant beef broth and 6 cups water
2 large potatoes, pared and diced
2 large onions, chopped (2 cups)
1 cup chopped celery
1 large carrot, pared and chopped
1 teaspoon caraway seeds, crushed
1 teaspoon salt
¼ teaspoon pepper

1 Melt shortening in a large skillet or a 5-quart electric slow cooker with a browning unit. Add beef cubes and stir over high heat for 5 minutes.
2 Add paprika and mix well. Stir in tomato purée. Pour into a 5-quart slow cooker; stir in CLASSIC BEEF BROTH or instant beef broth and water, potatoes, onions, celery, carrot, caraway seeds, salt and pepper; cover.
3 Cook on low (190° to 200°) 8 hours, or on high (290° to 300°) 4 hours. Taste and add additional salt and pepper, if you wish. Serve in heated soup bowls with pumpernickel bread and pickled beets.

Bonus Beef Soup

Never let beef bones go to waste: pack in plastic bags and freeze until you have enough to make this delicious soup

Cook on 190° to 200° for 10 hours,
or on 290° to 300° for 5 hours.
Makes 6 servings.

4 to 6 beef bones
8 cups water
1 can (1 pound) tomatoes
2 medium-size carrots, pared and chopped
1 white turnip, pared and chopped
1 large onion, chopped (1 cup)
1 cup chopped celery
1 bay leaf

2½ teaspoons salt
1 teaspoon leaf thyme, crumbled
¼ teaspoon pepper
1 cup elbow macaroni, cooked
1 cup chopped raw spinach

1 Combine beef bones, water, tomatoes, carrots, turnip, onion, celery, bay leaf, salt, thyme and pepper in an electric slow cooker; cover.
2 Cook on low (190° to 200°) 10 hours, or on high (290° to 300°) 5 hours.
3 Turn heat control to high (290° to 300°); stir in cooked macaroni and spinach; cook 10 minutes longer; taste and season with salt and pepper. Serve with rye bread and a Waldorf salad.

Potage Parmentier

This potato soup is named in honor of Antoine Parmentier who worked to make potatoes popular among the French

Cook on 190° to 200° for 8 hours,
or on 290° to 300° for 4 hours.
Makes 8 servings.

4 leeks, trimmed and sliced
1 large onion, chopped (1 cup)

No matter what the ingredient—cheese or onions, peppers or celery, meat or pasta, with crockery cooking you put the soup ingredients in when you are ready to leave and return when the soup is ready to eat.

¼ cup (½ stick) butter or margarine
4 large potatoes, pared and diced
6 cups CLASSIC CHICKEN BROTH (see index for recipe)
   OR: 6 envelopes or teaspoons instant chicken broth and 6 cups water
1 teaspoon salt
1 bay leaf
¼ teaspoon white pepper
2 cups light cream

1 Sauté leeks and onion in butter or margarine in a large skillet or 5-quart electric slow cooker with a browning unit until soft.
2 Combine with potatoes, CLASSIC CHICKEN BROTH or instant chicken broth and water, salt, bay leaf and pepper in a 5-quart slow cooker; cover.
3 Cook on low (190° to 200°) 8 hours, or on high (290° to 300°) 4 hours. Remove and discard bay leaf. Stir in cream; taste and add additional salt and pepper, if desired. Heat 15 minutes before serving.
Hostess Tip: This is the origin of VICHYSSOISE. To make VICHYSSOISE: Cool soup slightly; then process, a few cups at a time, in an electric blender container until smooth. Pour into a glass bowl and chill thoroughly. Serve in chilled bowls with a sprinkling of chopped chives.

Old-Fashioned Lentil Soup

Ham bone plus the last meaty pickings from it go into this thick hearty soup

Cook on 190° to 200° for 10 hours,
or on 290° to 300° for 5 hours.
Makes 6 servings.

1 ham bone (from baked ham)
6 cups water
1¼ cups dried lentils (from a 1-pound package)
4 medium-size carrots, pared and sliced
1 large onion, chopped (1 cup)
2 teaspoons salt
1 teaspoon sugar
¼ teaspoon pepper
1 bay leaf

1 Combine ham bone, water, lentils, carrots, onion, sugar, salt, pepper and bay leaf in an electric slow cooker; cover.
2 Cook on low (190° to 200°) 10 hours, or on high (290° to 300°) 5 hours.
3 Take out ham bone; strip off bits of meat and add to soup. Remove bay leaf.
4 Ladle soup into heated serving bowls.

Philadelphia Pepper Pot

A tripe soup that is said to go back to the time of George Washington

Cook on 190° to 200° for 8 hours,
or on 290° to 300° for 4 hours.
Makes 8 servings.

½ cup diced salt pork
3 leeks, trimmed and chopped
1 medium-size onion, chopped (½ cup)
3 green peppers, halved, seeded and chopped
1 cup chopped celery
1 tablespoon all-purpose flour
1 cup diced parboiled tripe
2 medium-size potatoes, pared and diced
3 small tomatoes, peeled and chopped
8 cups CLASSIC BEEF BROTH (see index for recipe)
  OR: 8 envelopes or teaspoons instant beef broth and 8 cups water
1 tablespoon salt
½ teaspoon freshly ground pepper
1 bay leaf
¼ teaspoon leaf thyme, crumbled

1 Brown salt pork in a large skillet or an electric slow cooker with a browning unit; remove and reserve.
2 Sauté leeks, onion, green peppers and celery in pan drippings until soft; stir in flour and cook 2 minutes.
3 Combine mixture with salt pork and tripe in an electric slow cooker. Add potatoes, tomatoes, CLASSIC BEEF BROTH or instant beef broth and water, salt, pepper, bay leaf and thyme; cover.
4 Cook on low (190° to 200°) 8 hours, or on high (290° to 300°) 4 hours, or until broth is rich and flavorful. Remove bay leaf. Taste and season with salt and pepper. Serve with refrigerated flaky biscuits and a hearty Burgundy, if you wish.

Scotch Lamb Broth

The last of a leg of lamb can be substituted for the lamb combination

Cook on 190° to 200° for 10 hours,
or on 290° to 300° for 5 hours.
Makes 8 servings.

2 pounds lamb shoulder combination
2 leeks, trimmed and sliced
2 cups chopped celery
2 large carrots, pared and chopped
1 medium-size onion, chopped
8 cups water
2 teaspoons salt
½ teaspoon pepper
½ cup pearl barley
1 cup light cream

1 Trim excess fat from lamb. Place in an electric slow cooker with leeks, celery, carrots, onion, water, salt and pepper. Stir in pearl barley; cover.
2 Cook on low (190° to 200°) 10 hours, or on high (290° to 300°) 5 hours, or until meat is tender and barley is cooked. Stir in cream just before serving.

Pot Au Feu

Serve this very French soup in deep bowls with toasted French bread and a big salad

Cook on 190° to 200° for 8 hours,
or on 290° to 300° for 4 hours.
Makes 8 servings.

1 bottom round roast (about 3 pounds)
1 marrow bone, cracked
4 cups cold water
4 large carrots, pared and sliced
4 medium-size onions, peeled and sliced
3 potatoes, pared and diced
3 white turnips, pared and diced
2 cups sliced celery
1 small parsnip, pared and diced
¼ cup chopped parsley
2 teaspoons salt

1 Trim excess fat from beef; cut into 3 or 4 pieces. Place in electric slow cooker with marrow bone and water.
2 Add carrots, onions, potatoes, turnips, celery, parsnip, parsley and salt; cover slow cooker.
3 Cook on low (190° to 200°) 8 hours, or on high (290° to 300°) 4 hours, or until beef and vegetables are very tender. Remove beef and marrow bone from slow cooker; disconnect cooker; drop a few ice cubes into broth. (If your slow cooker is crockery, you might prefer to pour broth into a large metal bowl before adding ice cubes to avoid damage due to temperature change.)

4 Cut beef into small pieces; skim fat from top of broth; return beef and broth (if removed from cooker) to cooker; taste and season with salt and pepper.

5 Turn heat control to high (290° to 300°); cover; heat 30 minutes or until soup is steamy-hot. Ladle into heated deep bowls and serve at once.

Suggested Variations: Try substituting leeks for the onion in this recipe; peeled tomatoes add a new touch; green beans and peas give a springtime flavor to the soup. Note: If you are in a hurry at dinner time, reheat soup in a metal saucepan on top of the range. Soup also freezes well.

Old-Fashioned Beef and Vegetable Soup

This hearty soup, chock-full of vegetables and meat, is a meal in itself

Cook on 190° to 200° for 8 hours,
or on 290° to 300° for 4 hours.
Makes 8 servings.

6 cups BASIC BEEF BROTH (see index for recipe)
2 large potatoes, peeled and diced (2 cups)
2 large carrots, pared and sliced
1 cup sliced celery
2 small onions, peeled and quartered
1 can (1 pound) whole tomatoes
2 teaspoons salt
⅛ teaspoon pepper
½ head green cabbage, shredded (2 cups)
1 cup frozen corn (from a plastic bag), thawed
3 cups diced cooked beef
1 tablespoon chopped parsley

1 Combine BASIC BEEF BROTH in slow cooker with potatoes, carrots, celery, onions, tomatoes, salt and pepper.

2 Cook on low (190° to 200°) 8 hours, or on high (290° to 300°) 4 hours.

3 Stir in cabbage, corn and meat; turn heat control to high (290° to 300°) and cook 15 minutes longer or just until all vegetables are crisply tender. Sprinkle with parsley.

4 Ladle into soup bowls. Serve with chunks of crusty bread.

DUMPLING MAGIC

Dumplings can be made successfully in your slow cooker if you follow these directions:

● *Use a recipe that has at least 1 teaspoon baking powder to each cup of sifted all-purpose flour.*

● *The slow cooker should be at least ¾ full and the level of the liquid should not be above the level of the food. If the liquid is above the food, remove excess liquid from cooker with a bulb baster before dropping dumpling batter onto food. (Excess liquid can prevent dumplings from cooking completely.)*

● *Dumplings can either be cooked for 30 minutes on high (290° to 300°) with the cooker covered, or cooked on high (290° to 300°) 15 minutes uncovered, then 15 minutes covered.*

Turkey Broth

A great way to get extra mileage from your holiday birds

Cook on 190° to 200° for 8 hours,
or on 290° to 300° for 4 hours.
Makes approximately 12 servings.

1 turkey carcass
1 large onion, sliced
1 large carrot, sliced
¼ cup celery tops
1 tablespoon salt
¼ teaspoon pepper
Water
¼ teaspoon monosodium glutamate

1 Break turkey carcass into pieces small enough to fit into your slow cooker; add onion, carrot, celery tops, salt, pepper, monosodium glutamate, enough water to cover. Cover slow cooker.

2 Cook on low (190° to 200°) 8 hours, or on high (290° to 300°) 4 hours. Cool.

3 When cool enough to handle, lift out turkey carcass, remove any bits of meat and chop coarsely. Strain broth; add meat, cool, then skim fat from top. Reheat and serve immediately or store in freezer for use later.

Classic Beef Broth

Slow cookers are taking the place of the old soup pot which simmered for hours on the back of a wood-burning stove

Bake at 450° for 40 minutes.
Cook on 190° to 200° for 10 hours,
or on 290° to 300° for 5 hours.
Makes 12 cups.

3 pounds meaty beef bones
1 veal bone, cracked (optional)
3 large carrots, pared and chopped
2 large onions, halved
1 leek, trimmed
2 celery stalks with leaves, chopped
10 cups water
   Handful parsley
2 cloves garlic, peeled
1 tablespoon salt
1 bay leaf
3 whole cloves

1 Put the meat bones, carrots, onions, leek and celery into a roasting pan.
2 Roast in hot oven (450°) 40 minutes, or until bones are well browned.
3 Place browned bones and vegetables in a 5-quart electric slow cooker; add water, parsley, garlic, salt, bay leaf and cloves; cover cooker.
4 Cook on low (190° to 200°) 10 hours, or on high (290° to 300°) 5 hours, or until broth is rich and flavorful; strain broth through cheese-cloth into a large bowl.
5 Refrigerate broth, up to 4 days, leaving the fat layer on surface until ready to use; then lift off fat and discard. To freeze broth, pour into recipe-size plastic freezer containers to within ½-inch of top; seal; label and date. Freeze. Plan to use within 3 months.

LEFTOVERS FOR SOUP

• Meat, fish and poultry bones, left after cooking, can be used as the foundation of soups, sauces and stews.
• Add vegetables and fruit parings to the pot, too—you'll be surprised at the flavor they impart.

Minestrone

This version of an Italian favorite includes salami and garden vegetables

Cook on 190° to 200° for 8 hours,
or on 290° to 300° for 4 hours.
Makes 8 servings.

1 cup dried white beans (cannellini), from a 1-pound package
8 cups water
½ pound salami, diced
2 cups chopped celery
1 can (1 pound) tomatoes
4 cups shredded cabbage
2 large zucchini, trimmed and sliced
1 cup cubed, pared yellow turnip
¼ cup chopped parsley
1 teaspoon salt
1 teaspoon leaf basil, crumbled
½ cup elbow macaroni, cooked
   Grated Parmesan cheese

1 Pick over beans and rinse under running water. Combine beans and water in a large saucepan. Bring to boiling; cook 2 minutes; remove from heat; cover; let stand 1 hour. (Or combine beans and water in an electric slow cooker and let stand all night at room temperature.)
2 Combine beans and liquid with salami, celery, tomatoes, cabbage, zucchini, turnip, parsley, salt and basil in slow cooker; cover.
3 Cook on low (190° to 200°) 8 hours, or on high (290° to 300°) 4 hours; stir in cooked macaroni and cook 10 minutes.
4 Ladle into soup bowls; sprinkle with grated Parmesan cheese.

Old Farm Bean Soup

Mothers have known for generations that a bubbling pot of rich bean soup makes hearty family eating that's easy on the budget

Cook on 190° to 200° for 8 hours,
then on 290° to 300° for 4 hours.
Makes 8 servings.

1 package (1 pound) dried navy or pea beans
6 cups water
¼ pound salt pork
1 large onion, chopped (1 cup)
1 large carrot, pared and chopped
4 smoked sausage links, scored (from a 12-ounce package)

1 bay leaf
1½ teaspoons salt
½ teaspoon pepper
¼ teaspoon leaf thyme, crumbled

1 Pick over beans and rinse under running water. Combine beans and water in a large kettle. Bring to boiling; cover; cook 10 minutes. Remove from heat; let stand 1 hour. (Or soak beans in water in slow cooker overnight.)
2 Place beans and liquid in slow cooker, score salt pork, almost to rind; push down into beans; stir in onion, carrot, sausage links, bay leaf, salt, pepper and leaf thyme; cover.
3 Cook on low (190° to 200°) 8 hours; stir beans; turn heat control to high (290° to 300°) and cook for 4 hours; stir beans with a wooden spoon and mash some of them against the side of the cooker to thicken soup. Remove bay leaf. Taste beans; season with additional salt and pepper, if desired.

Borscht

A Russian favorite that is classically served with a dollop of sour cream

Cook on 190° to 200° for 8 hours,
or on 290° to 300° for 4 hours.
Makes 8 servings.

2 cups shredded cabbage
2 large onions, chopped (2 cups)
1 cup chopped celery
4 large beets, pared and shredded
2 large carrots, pared and shredded
3 tablespoons butter or margarine
2 pounds chicken wings
1 pound boneless chuck, cubed
10 cups water
1 can (6 ounces) tomato paste
2 teaspoons salt
¼ teaspoon pepper
    Dairy sour cream

1 Sauté cabbage, onions, celery, beets and carrots in butter or margarine in a large skillet or a 5-quart slow cooker with a browning unit.
2 Combine vegetables with chicken wings, cubed beef, water, tomato paste, salt and pepper in a 5-quart slow cooker; cover cooker.
3 Cook on low (190° to 200°) 8 hours, or on high (290° to 300°) 4 hours, or until soup is rich and flavorful. Taste and season with additional salt and pepper, if you wish.
4 Serve in heated soup bowls and top each serving with sour cream.

Garden Patch Soup

An easy-to-make soup that's ready to simmer in about 15 minutes

Cook on 190° to 200° for 5 hours,
or on 290° to 300° for 3 hours.
Makes 6 servings.

1 medium-size onion, chopped (½ cup)
2 medium-size potatoes, peeled and chopped
1 can (1 pound) whole-kernel corn, drained
1 package (10 ounces) frozen lima beans, thawed
2 cans (13¾ ounces each) chicken broth
1 can (26 ounces) tomato juice
1 cup diced cooked chicken
1½ teaspoons salt
¼ teaspoon pepper
1 tablespoon butter or margarine
1 tablespoon Worcestershire sauce

1 Combine onion, potatoes, corn, lima beans, chicken broth, tomato juice, chicken, salt, pepper, butter or margarine and Worcestershire sauce in a slow cooker; cover.
2 Cook on low (190° to 200°) 5 hours, or on high (290° to 300°) 3 hours. Serve with wedges of process American cheese and crackers for a complete meal.

Meat Ball Chowder

Tiny balls of mint-seasoned beef and pork cook in a rich onion broth

Cook on 190° to 200° for 8 hours,
or on 290° to 300° for 4 hours.
Makes 6 servings.

¾ pound ground chuck
¾ pound ground pork
1 egg
2 teaspoons dried mint leaves, crumbled
1½ teaspoons salt
¼ teaspoon pepper
4 cups boiling water
1 envelope (2 to a package) onion soup mix
1 can (1 pound) stewed tomatoes
1 can (1 pound) red kidney beans
¼ cup chopped parsley

1 Mix ground beef and pork with egg, mint leaves, salt and pepper in a bowl; shape into tiny balls.

(continued)

2 Pour boiling water into an electric slow cooker; stir in onion soup mix, meat balls, stewed tomatoes and kidney beans with liquid; cover.
3 Cook on low (190° to 200°) 8 hours, or on high (290° to 300°) 4 hours; stir parsley into hot soup.
4 Ladle into soup bowls; serve with chowder crackers, if you wish.

SOUPS CLEAR AND THIN

Hot Spiced Tomato Cup

Serve this tangy dinner starter in dainty cups with a crisp nibble

Makes 12 servings

2 *bottles (1 pint, 10 ounces each) tomato-juice
   cocktail*
½ *teaspoon ground allspice*
1 *lemon, cut in 12 thin slices*

1 Mix tomato-juice cocktail and allspice in a large saucepan; heat, stirring several times, to boiling.
2 Pour into small cups; float a slice of lemon on each. Serve hot.

Tomato Consommé

An all-purpose soup; serve as an accompaniment to a sandwich, on a buffet, or as soup of the day

Makes 8 servings

2 *cups water*
4 *beef-bouillon cubes
   Handful of celery leaves*
1 *medium-size onion, peeled and sliced*
¼ *cup chopped parsley*

There's a reason why everyone has tasted **Tomato Consommé.** Quite simply, it is so good it is served everywhere.

1 teaspoon salt
½ teaspoon leaf basil, crumbled
2 bay leaves
1 can (46 ounces) tomato juice

1 Combine water, bouillon cubes, celery leaves, onion, parsley, salt, basil and bay leaves in a large saucepan; heat to boiling, then simmer 15 minutes.
2 Stir in tomato juice; heat 5 minutes longer, or until bubbly-hot. Strain into heated soup bowls or cups.

Bouillon Imperial

Once this soup was reserved for the sick—now it is enjoyed by everyone

Makes 6 servings

2 cans (10½ ounces each) condensed beef broth
1 cup water
½ cup thinly sliced celery
½ cup thinly sliced radishes

1 Combine beef broth, water and celery in a medium-size saucepan; heat to boiling; cover. Simmer 10 minutes, or just until celery is crisply tender.
2 Ladle into soup bowls or cups; float radish slices on top. Serve with crisp thin wheat crackers, if you wish.

Sherried Mushroom Bouillon

Rich in flavor—no wonder it's enjoyed by kings

Makes 4 servings

1 can (3 or 4 ounces) sliced mushrooms
3 green onions, trimmed and sliced thin
1 tablespoon lemon juice
1 can (10½ ounces) condensed beef broth
1⅓ cups water
1 tablespoon dry sherry

1 Combine mushrooms and liquid, green onions and lemon juice in a medium-size saucepan. Heat to boiling; cover. Simmer 3 minutes.
2 Stir in beef broth and water. Heat to boiling. Turn off heat, stir in sherry.
3 Pour into soup cups; sprinkle with chopped parsley, if you wish.

Harvest Bouillon

Beef broth, apple cider, and lemon slices combine in this harvest-moon special

Makes 8 servings

2 cans (10½ ounces each) condensed beef broth
⅔ cup apple cider
⅔ cup water
2 tablespoons lemon juice
8 paper-thin slices of lemon
Parsley

1 Combine bouillon, apple cider, water and lemon juice in pitcher; chill.
2 At serving time, pour into glasses or punch cups and garnish with lemon slices and parsley.

Herbed Chicken Consommé

A cold soup for a warm day

Makes 8 servings

3 cans (13¾ ounces each) chicken broth
1 teaspoon leaf tarragon, crumbled
½ teaspoon leaf thyme, crumbled
1 small lemon, sliced
1 small onion, peeled and sliced
4 peppercorns
2 envelopes unflavored gelatin
2 cups (16-ounce carton) dairy sour cream

1 Pour broth into a large saucepan; skim off fat, if any.
2 Stir tarragon, thyme, lemon, onion and peppercorns into broth; sprinkle gelatin over top; let stand several minutes to soften gelatin.
3 Heat slowly to boiling; simmer 5 minutes; strain into a large shallow pan. Cool, then chill at least 2 hours, or until firm.
4 Just before serving, cut gelatin into tiny cubes; spoon cubes, alternately with sour cream, into parfait glasses. Garnish each with a sprig of parsley, if you wish.

When pool-side, load up a lifesaver with a collection of different cold *or* hot soups, and serve in colorful mugs.

Clear Turkey Noodle Soup

It's rich with homemade noodles—a real farm-style main-dish-of-the-meal

Makes 8 generous servings

12 cups TURKEY BROTH *(recipe follows)*
 2 cups diced celery
 1 small onion, chopped *(¼ cup)*
 1 teaspoon salt
 ¼ teaspoon pepper
   HOMEMADE EGG NOODLES *(recipe follows)*
   OR: 1 package (1 pound) wide egg noodles
 ¼ cup chopped parsley

1 Heat TURKEY BROTH, celery, onion, salt and pepper to boiling in large kettle. Drop in noodles, a few at a time, so broth does not stop boiling. Cook, stirring often, 10 minutes, or just until noodles are tender.
2 Stir in parsley; ladle into soup plates or big bowls.

TURKEY BROTH

Makes about 12 cups

Break turkey carcass enough to fit into a large kettle; add 1 sliced onion, 1 sliced carrot, handful of celery tops, 1 tablespoon salt, ¼ teaspoon pepper and water almost to cover (about 12 cups). Cover kettle; heat to boiling, then simmer 1 hour. Lift out carcass and, when cool enough to handle, remove any bits of meat and chop coarsely. Strain broth; add meat; cool, then chill enough to skim fat from top. If you plan to use it within a few days, store in covered jars in refrigerator; if to be used later, freeze in freezer containers.

Homemade Egg Noodles

If you have never made them, do try this easy recipe. Dough needs to dry, so mix it about 2 hours before cooking time

Makes about 1 pound uncooked noodles

 4 eggs
 1 teaspoon salt
 2½ cups sifted all-purpose flour

(continued)

1 Beat eggs well with salt in medium-size bowl. Stir in 1 cup flour, then mix in enough of remaining 1½ cups to make a stiff dough. (It should be slightly stiffer than piecrust dough.)
2 Turn out on floured pastry cloth or board; knead a few times to make dough smooth. Shape into a ball; cover with a clean tea towel; let rest on pastry cloth or board about 30 minutes.
3 Roll out half the dough into a large thin sheet; carefully roll sheet around rolling pin, then unroll and hang dough on tea towel spread on a rod or over back of straight-back chair (a broom handle set on the backs of 2 chairs makes a good rod). Repeat with remaining dough; let dough hang 30 minutes, or until dry but still pliable.
4 Roll up each sheet, jelly-roll fashion. Cut into ½-inch slices. Separate and unroll strips. Spread out on board to let dry, turning occasionally, about 30 minutes. Noodles are now ready to be cooked.

Old-Time Lemon Soup

It's cool and tangy, with the fresh spark only lemon can add

Makes 4 to 6 servings

1 envelope chicken-noodle–soup mix
1 cup thinly sliced celery
4 teaspoons lemon juice
2 hard-cooked eggs, finely diced

1 Prepare soup mix, following label directions; cook 5 minutes; add celery and cook 2 minutes longer.
2 Remove from heat; stir in lemon juice; pour into bowl; cover; chill.
3 Serve in cups or small bowls, with diced hard-cooked eggs to be sprinkled over.

Greek Lemon Soup

Another time, chill before serving

Makes 6 to 8 servings

2 cans (10¾ ounces each) condensed chicken broth
2 soup cans of water
⅓ cup uncooked regular rice
4 eggs
2 tablespoons lemon juice

1 Combine chicken broth and water in a large saucepan; heat to boiling. Stir in rice; cover. Cook 20 minutes, or until rice is tender; remove from heat.
2 Beat eggs until frothy-light in a medium-size bowl; slowly beat in lemon juice, then 1 cup of the hot broth mixture; beat back into remaining broth mixture in saucepan. Heat slowly, stirring several times, just until hot. (Do not boil.)
3 Ladle into heated soup bowls or cups; sprinkle with parsley, if you wish.

Jellied Bouillon Julienne

For a flavor variation, heat this vegetable soup

Makes 6 servings

2 cans (10½ ounces each) condensed beef consommé, chilled
1 small stalk celery
½ small carrot, pared
6 radishes, washed and trimmed
½ small cucumber, pared
1 green onion, trimmed

1 Empty jellied consommé into a medium-size bowl; keep in refrigerator while cutting up vegetables.
2 Cut celery, carrot, radishes and cucumber into 1-inch-long strips; slice green onion thin; fold into consommé.
3 Chill, stirring once or twice, at least 1 hour before serving.

Jellied Lemon Strata

Save this hot-weather soup for a special occasion

Makes 4 servings

1 envelope unflavored gelatin
1 can (13¾ ounces) chicken broth
1 teaspoon grated lemon peel
2 tablespoons lemon juice
¼ teaspoon salt
2 hard-cooked eggs, shelled
2 tablespoons chopped parsley

1 Soften gelatin in 1 cup of the chicken broth in a small saucepan; heat, stirring constantly, until gelatin dissolves; remove from heat.
2 Stir in remaining chicken broth, lemon peel

and juice and salt; pour into a baking dish, 9x9x2. Chill several hours.

3 Chop eggs coarsely; toss with parsley in a small bowl.

4 Cut gelatin mixture lengthwise and crosswise into ¼-inch cubes; spoon half into tall cups or parfait glasses. Top with egg mixture, then remaining gelatin mixture. Garnish each serving with a sprig of parsley, if you wish.

MAKE THE MOST OF VEGETABLE SOUPS

Black Bean Soup

This soup is a take-off on the exotic Brazilian *Feijoada*. Tangy pieces of orange complement bits of hot pepperoni in a deep dark bean stock

Makes 12 servings

> 4 cups dried black turtle beans (from two 1-pound bags)
> 3½ quarts water
> ½ pound pepperoni, cut into ½-inch pieces
> 3 large onions, sliced (3 cups)
> 1 boneless smoked pork butt (about 2 pounds)
> 2 cups dry red wine
> 3 oranges, peeled and sectioned
> 2 teaspoons salt
> ¼ cup chopped parsley

1 Combine beans with water in a large kettle; heat to boiling and boil 2 minutes; cover. Remove from heat; let stand 1 hour.

2 Heat beans to boiling again; add pepperoni and onions; reduce heat; cover. Simmer 2 hours, stirring occasionally, or until beans are tender. Add pork and wine. Simmer 1¼ hours longer, or until meat is cooked through.

3 Remove meat and keep warm. With a slotted spoon, remove pieces of sausage and about 3 cups of whole beans. Purée remaining beans in soup in a blender or press through a sieve. Return to kettle along with sausage and the whole beans.

4 Add sections from 2 of the oranges and salt. Taste; add additional salt, if you wish. Bring to boiling; ladle into soup bowls. Garnish each serving with a section of reserved orange; sprinkle with parsley.

5 Slice pork butt thin and pass it around to eat, on a separate plate, with mustard and whole-wheat bread.

Note: This freezes well. (Freeze soup and meats separately.)

Curried Black Bean Soup

A touch of spice gives zest to this hot-weather cooler

Makes 4 to 6 servings

> 1 can (11 ounces) condensed black-bean soup
> 1⅓ cups cold water
> ¼ teaspoon curry powder
> ¼ teaspoon grated lemon peel

1 Combine all ingredients in an electric-blender container or in a bowl; beat until smooth. Chill.

2 Pour into chilled glasses or cups. Garnish with lemon slices and sieved hard-cooked egg, if you wish.

Supper Bean Soup

Simmer a meaty ham bone with a pound of limas for a great whole-meal soup

Makes 6 generous servings

> 1 pound dried large lima beans
> 7 cups water
> 1 meaty bone from baked ham
> 1 medium-size onion, diced (½ cup)
> 1 teaspoon salt
> ¼ teaspoon pepper
> 1 to 2 cups milk

1 Wash beans and pick over; combine with water in a kettle. Heat to boiling; cook 2 minutes; cover. Remove from heat; let stand 1 hour.

2 Add ham bone, onion, salt and pepper; heat to boiling again; cover tightly. Simmer 1½ hours, or until beans are tender.

3 Remove ham bone and cool until easy to handle. Strip off meat, removing any fat; dice meat; return to kettle.

4 Stir in 1 to 2 cups milk, depending on how thick you like soup; heat slowly to boiling.

5 Ladle into soup bowls; sprinkle with chopped parsley and serve with French bread, if you wish.

Old-Fashioned Lentil Soup

Ham bone plus the last meaty pickings from it go into this thick hearty soup

Makes 6 servings

    1 ham bone (from baked ham)
    6 cups water
    1¼ cups dried lentils (from a 1-pound package)
    4 medium-size carrots, pared and sliced
    1 large onion, chopped (1 cup)
    2 teaspoons salt
    1 teaspoon sugar
    ¼ teaspoon pepper
    1 bay leaf

1 Combine all ingredients in a kettle; cover. Heat to boiling, then simmer 1 hour, or until lentils are tender.
2 Take out ham bone; strip off bits of meat and add to soup. Remove bay leaf.
3 Ladle soup into heated serving bowls.

Onion Soup

This soup can be made ahead of time; reheat and add bread and cheese just before serving

Makes 6 servings

    4 large onions, sliced (1½ pounds)
    4 tablespoons (½ stick) butter or margarine
    6 cups BASIC BEEF STOCK (see index for recipe)
    2 teaspoons salt
    ¼ teaspoon pepper
    6 to 8 slices French bread, toasted
    ½ cup grated Parmesan cheese
    ¼ cup Gruyère or Swiss cheese

1 Sauté onion in butter or margarine in Dutch oven 15 minutes, or until lightly browned. Stir in BEEF STOCK, salt and pepper. Bring to boiling; reduce heat; cover; simmer 30 minutes.
2 Ladle soup into 6 ovenproof soup bowls or 12-ounce custard cups, or an 8-cup casserole. Lay bread slices on top, sprinkle with cheeses.
3 Heat in very hot oven (425°) 10 minutes, then place under preheated broiler and broil until top is bubbly and lightly browned.

Smoky Pea Potage

Handy canned soup is the starter to combine with smoky wieners and carrots

Makes 6 servings

    ½ pound (about 4) frankfurters, sliced ½ inch thick
    1 cup diced, pared carrots
    1 teaspoon salt
    1 teaspoon leaf marjoram, crumbled
    3 cups water
    2 cans (11¼ ounces each) condensed green-pea soup

1 Sauté frankfurters lightly in a kettle; stir in carrots, salt, marjoram and water; cover. Simmer 15 minutes, or until carrots are tender.
2 Stir in green-pea soup; simmer, stirring several times, 15 minutes longer to blend flavors.
3 Ladle into soup bowls; garnish with paper-thin slices of raw carrot, if you wish.

Potato Tureen Treat

Canned potato soup and cream-style corn blend in this so-good chowder

Makes 4 servings

    1 can (10¾ ounces) condensed cream of potato soup
    1 can (10½ ounces) condensed cream of potato soup
    1 can (8 ounces) cream-style corn
    1 cup evaporated milk (from a tall can)
    1 cup milk
    1 tablespoon grated onion
    1 teaspoon Worcestershire sauce
    ¼ teaspoon pepper
    1 tablespoon chopped parsley

Combine all ingredients except parsley; heat until bubbly hot. Pour into a tureen; sprinkle with parsley.

Mushroom Soup, Country Style

An appetizer-soup that goes well with a sandwich

Makes 4 servings

    2½ cups milk
    1 medium-size onion, finely chopped (½ cup)
    1 cup chopped fresh mushrooms

¼ teaspoon salt
¼ teaspoon celery salt
¼ teaspoon paprika

1 Scald milk and onion in top of 1½-quart double boiler.
2 Add mushrooms and seasonings; place over boiling water; cook about 20 minutes, or until mushrooms are tender.
3 Serve piping hot, with chopped parsley and mushroom slices, if desired.

Spinach Chowder

A vegetable chowder is satisfying—and this is one of the best

Makes 6 servings

1 package (10 ounces) frozen chopped spinach
2 cans (13 ounces each) vichyssoise
1 cup milk
2 envelopes instant chicken broth
 OR: 2 teaspoons granulated chicken bouillon
1 tablespoon instant minced onion
4 hard-cooked eggs, shelled and sliced

1 Combine frozen spinach, vichyssoise, milk, chicken broth and onion in large heavy saucepan or Dutch oven.
2 Heat *slowly*, stirring occasionally, about 20 minutes, or until spinach is thawed; cover. Simmer 5 minutes.
3 Ladle into soup bowls; garnish each with egg slices. Serve with cheese crackers, if you wish.

Tomato and Zucchini Soup

A sunny Mediterranean-style soup that also makes a sparkling jellied variation

Makes 6 servings.

1 medium-size onion, chopped
2 tablespoons olive or vegetable oil
2 small zucchini, finely diced
4 cups tomato juice
1 can (13¾ ounces) chicken broth
3 tablespoons lime juice
2 teaspoons Worcestershire sauce
1 teaspoon salt
1 teaspoon sugar
⅛ to ¼ teaspoon liquid red-pepper seasoning
2 tablespoons chopped parsley
 Lime slices

1 Sauté onion in oil in large saucepan until soft, about 5 minutes. Stir in zucchini; sauté 2 to 3 minutes. Add tomato juice, chicken broth, lime juice, Worcestershire, sugar, salt and pepper seasoning.
2 Heat to boiling; lower heat; cover. Simmer 5 minutes. Stir in 2 tablespoons chopped parsley. Serve hot in mugs; garnish with lime slices.

JELLIED SOUP

Soften 2 envelopes unflavored gelatin in ½ cup cold water 5 minutes; stir into hot soup. Cool completely; chill several hours or overnight until jellied. To serve, break up with a fork and spoon into chilled glasses or soup bowls. Garnish with chopped parsley and lime slices.

Spoon-Up Fresh Vegetable Soup

So full of flavor—serve large chunks of homemade bread to sop up the last drops

Makes about 12 cups

1 pound lean shin or chuck beef, cut in 1-inch cubes
1 beef knucklebone, cracked
6 cups water
2 cans (about 1 pound each) tomatoes
3 carrots, sliced
1 leek or onion, sliced
1 clove of garlic, minced
2 bay leaves
1 tablespoon sugar
2 teaspoons salt
2 cups chopped cabbage
1 cup sliced zucchini
1 cup cut-up green beans
1 cup broken macaroni
¼ cup chopped parsley
 Grated Parmesan cheese

1 Simmer beef and bone with water, tomatoes, carrots, leek or onion, garlic, bay leaves, sugar and salt in kettle about 3 hours; remove bone; cool slightly; skim off fat.
2 Add cabbage, zucchini, green beans and macaroni; cook 45 minutes longer, or until beans are tender; sprinkle with parsley; serve with grated cheese.

Tomato Freeze

Instead of your usual soup, accompany a warm sandwich with this version of a frappé

Makes 6 servings

```
6 large ripe tomatoes, chopped
1½ teaspoons salt
⅛ teaspoon pepper
⅛ teaspoon ground thyme
3 whole cloves
1 large bay leaf
½ teaspoon onion juice
1 tablespoon lemon juice
  Cucumber slices
```

1 Combine tomatoes, salt, pepper, thyme, cloves, bay leaf and onion juice in a medium-size saucepan. Heat to boiling; cover. Cook 20 minutes.
2 Press mixture through a fine sieve into a medium-size bowl; stir in lemon juice. Pour into a shallow pan, 9x9x2; freeze several hours, or until firm.
3 Just before serving, break up frozen soup; crush fine in an ice crusher or an electric blender. (Or place pieces in a double-thick transparent bag; crush with a mallet.)
4 Spoon into cups or small bowls; garnish each serving with several cucumber slices.

Easy Gazpacho

Here's a speedy version of popular Spanish gazpacho, with its variety of toppings

Makes 6 servings

```
1 can (10¾ ounces) condensed tomato soup
1 soup can of water
3½ cups mixed vegetable juice (from a 46-
  ounce can)
1 tablespoon lemon juice
1 teaspoon seasoned salt
¼ cup sliced pitted ripe olives
1 cup croutons
1 cup grated raw carrots
1 cup diced avocado
1 cup sliced green onions
```

1 Blend tomato soup, water, vegetable juice, lemon juice and seasoned salt in large bowl; chill several hours, as the soup tastes best when served frosty-cold.
2 To serve, pour soup into a big glass or pottery bowl; stir in ripe-olive slices. (If you have a second larger bowl, partly fill with crushed ice

and set soup bowl in it to keep chilly-cold. Surround with smaller bowls of croutons, carrots, avocado and green onions. Spoon soup into serving cups; let each person add the topping he likes best.

Alpine Tomato Appetizer

Your helpers for this nippy starter: Dip mix and canned colorful mixed vegetables

Makes 6 servings

```
1 envelope unflavored gelatin
3 cups tomato juice (from a 46-ounce can)
1 envelope (about 1 tablespoon) onion-dip mix
1 can (1 pound) mixed vegetables, drained
½ cup chopped green pepper
6 tablespoons dairy sour cream
```

1 Combine gelatin and 1 cup tomato juice in small saucepan; heat slowly, stirring constantly, just until gelatin dissolves. Pour into medium-size bowl.
2 Stir in remaining tomato juice, dip mix, vegetables and green pepper. Chill about 2 hours, or until set. (Mixture will be soft.)
3 Spoon into individual serving dishes; top each with 1 tablespoon sour cream and a green-pepper twist, if you wish. (To make: Shave paper-thin strips from cut edge of a green pepper with a vegetable parer; tie each into a loose knot.)

Double Tomato Soup

What better way to top off an evening than with a simple sandwich and this soup

Makes 4 servings

```
1 medium-size onion, chopped (½ cup)
2 tablespoons butter or margarine
3 medium-size tomatoes, diced (about 2 cups)
½ cup diced celery
1 can (10¾ ounces) condensed tomato soup
1 soup can water
1 teaspoon sugar
½ teaspoon salt
½ teaspoon leaf basil, crumbled
⅛ teaspoon pepper
```

1 Sauté onion in butter or margarine until soft in medium-size saucepan.
2 Stir in remaining ingredients; heat to boiling.

Simmer, uncovered, stirring once or twice, 10 minutes, to blend flavors.

3 Spoon into heated soup bowls; float a few croutons on top of each, if you wish.

Cheese and Vegetable Chowder

Make the portions large and you have a meal-in-one

Makes 6 servings

4 medium-size potatoes, pared and diced (3 cups)
1 medium-size onion, chopped (½ cup)
3 large stalks celery, trimmed and sliced thin
2 large carrots, pared and sliced thin
¼ green pepper, seeded and chopped
2½ cups water
2 teaspoons salt
Dash of pepper
2 cups milk
1 package (8 ounces) process American cheese, shredded (2 cups)
3 frankfurters, sliced thin
Paprika

1 Combine potatoes, onion, celery, carrots, green pepper, water, salt and pepper in a kettle; heat to boiling; cover. Simmer 20 minutes, or until vegetables are tender.

2 Stir in milk, cheese and frankfurters. Heat slowly, stirring constantly, until cheese melts.

3 Ladle into heated soup bowls or plates; sprinkle each with paprika.

Creamy Corn Chowder

An all-time American favorite, corn chowder has a place on every table

Makes 2 quarts

¼ pound lean salt pork
1 large onion, chopped (1 cup)
1 cup diced celery
2 tablespoons butter or margarine
1 cup water
2 cans (about 1 pound each) cream-style corn
2 cups fresh milk
1 large can (14 ounces) evaporated milk
¼ teaspoon salt
Dash of pepper

1 Dice salt pork finely; sauté slowly in kettle 15 minutes, or until crisp and golden; spoon from

kettle with slotted spoon; drain on paper towels; save for Step 3. Pour all fat from kettle, but do not wash kettle.

2 Sauté onion and celery in butter or margarine in same kettle for 5 minutes; add water; cover; simmer 5 minutes.

3 Stir in corn, fresh and evaporated milk, cooked salt pork, salt and pepper. (Salt pork varies in saltiness, so season lightly until you have tasted chowder.)

4 Heat chowder just to boiling; serve with buttered toasted pilot or unsalted plain crackers.

Duchess Vegetable Soup

Garden-fresh sweet peas add color and crunch to creamy-rich cheese soup from a can

Makes 6 servings

1 medium-size onion, chopped (½ cup)
1 cup diced celery
2 tablespoons butter or margarine
2½ cups water
2 tablespoons instant mashed potato (from a package)
1 pound fresh peas, shelled (1 cup)
1 can (11 ounces) condensed Cheddar cheese soup
⅛ teaspoon pepper
1 teaspoon Worcestershire sauce

1 Sauté onion and celery in butter or margarine until softened in medium-size saucepan; stir in water; heat to boiling.

2 Stir in instant mashed potato until blended, then add peas. Cover; cook 5 minutes. Stir in remaining ingredients until well blended; heat just to boiling.

3 Pour into mugs or soup bowls; float a few fluffs of popped corn on each serving for a snowy garnish, if you wish.

Garden Salad-Soup

Drink your salad as a cold summer soup. Also good hot on a rainy day

Makes 6 servings

1 *small onion, chopped (¼ cup)*
½ *teaspoon leaf basil, crumbled*
2 *tablespoons butter or margarine*
1 *cup water*
2 *teaspoons instant chicken bouillon*
   OR: 2 chicken-bouillon cubes
1 *teaspoon sugar*
1 *teaspoon Worcestershire sauce*
2 *cups finely chopped romaine or iceberg lettuce*
1 *cup finely chopped cabbage*
1 *cup finely chopped spinach*
3 *cups tomato juice (from a 46-ounce can)*

1 Sauté onion with basil in butter or margarine until soft in medium-size saucepan; stir in water, instant chicken bouillon or cubes, sugar and Worcestershire sauce; heat, stirring until bouillon is dissolved; remove from heat.
2 Combine remaining ingredients in large bowl; stir in bouillon mixture; chill.

Vegetable Minestrone

Add a small amount of your favorite cooked pasta for a meal in a bowl

Makes 4 to 6 servings

1 *envelope (2½ ounces) tomato-vegetable soup mix*
3 *cups boiling water*
1 *medium-size onion, chopped (½ cup)*
1 *can (about 1 pound) red kidney beans*
1 *can (12 to 16 ounces) whole-kernel corn*
1 *can (8 ounces) tomato sauce*
1 *teaspoon salt*
⅛ *teaspoon pepper*
½ *cup chopped parsley*
   Grated Parmesan cheese

1 Stir soup mix into boiling water in large saucepan; add onion, kidney beans, corn, tomato sauce, salt and pepper; cover.
2 Heat to boiling; cook 10 minutes, or until onion is tender; stir in parsley; serve in mugs or bowls with a generous sprinkling of Parmesan cheese.

El Rancho Soup

Beans, corn, and pimiento make this Southwest soup one you'll enjoy

Makes 4 servings

1 *tablespoon butter or margarine*
1 *small onion, chopped*
1 *cup Frenched green beans, cut in 1-inch pieces*
¼ *teaspoon sugar*
1 *can (10¾ ounces) chicken noodle soup*
1 *can (10½ ounces) condensed beef bouillon*
2 *soup cans of water*
2 *tablespoons chopped parsley*
1 *pimiento, diced*
1 *ear of corn, cut in 1-inch-thick slices*

1 Melt butter or margarine in large saucepan; add onion, beans and sugar; sauté over low heat 2 to 3 minutes, stirring often.
2 Stir in soups, water, parsley, pimiento and corn; heat to boiling; simmer 5 minutes, or until beans are cooked tender-crisp.

BOLD MAIN-DISH SOUPS AND CHOWDERS

Boothbay Chowder

Clams are the essential ingredient in this thick main-dish soup

Makes 6 to 8 servings

3 *slices bacon, chopped*
1 *large onion, chopped (1 cup)*
4 *medium-size potatoes, pared and diced (3 cups)*
2 *cups water*
1 *teaspoon salt*
¼ *teaspoon pepper*
2 *cans (10½ ounces each) minced clams*
1 *bottle (8 ounces) clam juice*
1 *cup light cream or table cream*
3 *tablespoons all-purpose flour*
2 *tablespoons minced parsley*

(continued)

New England is famous for chowders, and **Boothbay Chowder** made with clams, potatoes, onions, bacon, parsley, and cream is one of its best.

1 Cook bacon until crisp in a large heavy saucepan or Dutch oven. Remove bacon with slotted spoon; drain on paper toweling; reserve. Add onion to bacon drippings in saucepan; sauté until soft.
2 Add potatoes, water, salt and pepper; cover. Simmer, 15 minutes, or until potatoes are tender. Remove from heat.
3 Drain liquid from clams into a 4-cup measure; reserve clams. Add bottled clam juice and cream.
4 Briskly stir flour into clam liquid in cup. Add to potato mixture in saucepan. Cook, stirring constantly, over medium heat, until chowder thickens and bubbles 1 minute.
5 Add clams; heat just until piping-hot. Ladle into soup bowls. Sprinkle with parsley and reserved bacon. Serve with pilot crackers, if you wish.

Oyster Chowder

This dish is one you'll not soon forget

Makes 6 generous servings

1 can (1 pound) small white potatoes. drained and diced
4 tablespoons (½ stick) butter or margarine
2 cans (10½ ounces each) condensed oyster stew
1 can (1 pound) green peas
1 can (12 or 16 ounces) whole-kernel corn
1 can (5 ounces) lobster meat, drained and diced
2 cups milk
2 tablespoons instant minced onion
1 teaspoon salt
1 teaspoon Worcestershire sauce
Few drops liquid red pepper seasoning
Chopped parsley

1 Sauté potatoes lightly in butter or margarine in a kettle.
2 Stir in oyster stew, peas and corn and liquids, lobster, milk, onion, salt, Worcestershire sauce and red pepper seasoning; heat very slowly just to boiling. (Do not let chowder boil.)
3 Ladle into a tureen or heated soup bowls: sprinkle with chopped parsley. Serve with thin bread sticks, slices of crusty bread or your favorite crackers, if you wish.

Hungarian Paprika Soup-Stew

The highest grade paprika comes from Hungary—so buy the best when you make this colorful soup-stew

Makes 4 servings.

1 large onion, chopped (1 cup)
2 tablespoons vegetable oil
1 pound ground chuck
½ teaspoon salt
1 tablespoon paprika
¼ teaspoon black pepper
1 can (10½ ounces) condensed vegetable soup
1 can (10¾ ounces) condensed cream of potato soup
1 soup-can of water

1 Sauté onion in oil in a large saucepan. Add beef, breaking up with wooden spoon; cook 3 minutes or until all pink has disappeared from meat. Stir in salt, paprika and pepper.
2 Combine soups and water in a 4-cup measure; pour over meat and onions; stir well. Bring to boiling; lower heat. Cook 5 minutes, stirring constantly. Serve with crusty bread.

Crab-Cheese Chowder

A full-bodied soup for a meal to remember

Makes 4 to 6 servings

1½ tablespoons butter or margarine
1 onion, thinly sliced
2 stalks of celery, thinly sliced
3 cups diced raw potatoes
½ cup water
1 teaspoon salt
¼ teaspoon pepper
¼ pound process cheese
1 can (about 6 ounces) crabmeat, boned and flaked
3 cups milk, scalded
1 tablespoon chopped parsley

1 Melt butter or margarine in large saucepan; add onion and celery; cook slowly until golden; add potatoes, water, salt and pepper; simmer 15 to 20 minutes, or until potatoes are tender.
2 Slice in cheese; add crabmeat, milk and parsley; heat slowly until cheese melts. For a party touch, sprinkle more chopped parsley in wreath on top.

At your next Sunday brunch, impress family and guests with **Summer Fish Chowder**—a full blending of cod, lobster, clams, corn, green peas, and milk.

Summer Fish Chowder

It's a seafood fan's dream with cod, whole clams and lobster, plus two vegetables

Makes 6 servings

1 large onion, chopped (1 cup)
3 tablespoons butter or margarine
1 package (1 pound) frozen cod fillets
1 package (10 ounces) frozen peas
2 cups water
2 teaspoons salt
¼ teaspoon pepper
¼ teaspoon leaf thyme, crumbled

1 can (about 5 ounces) lobster meat
2 cans (about 10 ounces each) whole clams
1 can (1 pound) cream-style corn
1 can (14 ounces) evaporated milk
Chopped parsley

1 Sauté onion in butter or margarine until soft in a kettle; add frozen cod, peas, water, salt, pepper and thyme; cover. Heat to boiling, then simmer, breaking cod into large flakes as it thaws, 15 minutes.
2 While fish simmers, drain lobster; remove bony tissue, if any, then cut meat into large pieces.
3 Stir into fish mixture in kettle with clams and
(continued)

broth, corn and evaporated milk; cover. Heat slowly just to boiling.
4 Ladle into heated soup bowls and sprinkle with chopped parsley.

Classic Oyster Stew

The Yankee way with stew—and so easy to make!

Makes 4 servings

2 cups milk
2 cups light cream or table cream
½ teaspoon salt
¼ teaspoon paprika
1 pint (about 24) oysters
 OR: 2 cans (7 ounces each) frozen oysters, thawed
4 tablespoons (½ stick) butter or margarine

1 Scald milk with cream in medium-size saucepan over low heat (do not boil); stir in salt and paprika.
2 Heat oysters and juice in butter or margarine until edges of oysters begin to curl in medium-size saucepan; stir in scalded-milk mixture.
3 Ladle into heated soup bowls or mugs. Serve with oyster crackers, if you wish.

Creole Fish Soup

If you can readily buy fresh fish, use instead of frozen and substitute cayenne pepper (add to taste, after cooking) for chili

Makes 5 cups

1 small onion, sliced
½ cup sliced celery
1 teaspoon chili powder
1 tablespoon olive oil
2 cans (8 ounces each) tomato sauce
1 cup water
1 teaspoon salt
1 teaspoon sugar
¼ teaspoon Worcestershire sauce
1 package (12 ounces) frozen fish fillets (cod, sole, haddock, perch, whiting)
2 cups hot cooked rice
2 tablespoons chopped parsley

1 Sauté onion, celery and chili powder lightly in oil in large saucepan 10 minutes; stir in tomato sauce, water, salt, sugar and Worcestershire sauce; heat to boiling.

2 Add frozen fish in one piece; simmer, separating it with a fork as it thaws, 15 minutes, or until it flakes easily.
3 Spoon into chowder bowls; top each with a mound of rice mixed with parsley.

Tureen Shrimp

Canned potato soup, shrimp, and cheese go into this company-like surprise

Makes 6 servings

1 large onion, chopped (1 cup)
2 tablespoons butter or margarine
2 cans (10¾ ounces each) condensed cream of potato soup
3½ cups milk
1 package (1 pound) frozen deveined shelled raw shrimp
½ cup grated American cheese
2 tablespoons chopped parsley

1 Sauté onion in butter or margarine until soft in a kettle; stir in potato soup and milk.
2 Heat to boiling; stir in frozen shrimp; heat to boiling again, then simmer, stirring several times, 25 minutes, or just until shrimps are tender. Remove from heat.
3 Just before serving, stir in grated cheese until melted. Ladle into soup bowls; sprinkle with parsley.

Tureen Salmon

This is an expensive recipe—so save it for when company is special

Makes 8 generous servings

3 medium-size potatoes, pared and diced (1½ cups)
1 large onion, chopped (1 cup)
1 cup thinly sliced celery
4 tablespoons (½ stick) butter or margarine
⅓ cup sifted all-purpose flour
6 cups milk
1 bag (2 pounds) frozen peas and carrots
2 cans (1 pound each) salmon
1 teaspoon dillweed
1½ teaspoons salt
¼ teaspoon seasoned pepper
 Chowder crackers

1 Cook potatoes, covered, in boiling water to

cover in a medium-size saucepan 15 minutes, or just until tender; set aside.

2 Sauté onion and celery in butter or margarine until soft in a kettle. Blend in flour; cook, stirring constantly, until bubbly. Stir in milk; continue cooking and stirring until mixture thickens and boils 1 minute.

3 Stir in peas and carrots; heat slowly to boiling; cover. Simmer 12 minutes, or until vegetables are tender.

4 Drain salmon; remove skin and bones; break salmon into large chunks. Stir into vegetable mixture with potatoes and liquid, dillweed, salt and pepper. Heat slowly, stirring several times, just until hot.

5 Ladle into a tureen or heated soup bowls or plates; sprinkle with more dillweed, if you wish, and serve with chowder crackers.

Tomato-Tuna Treat

Accompany with crackers or large chunks of homemade bread

Makes 6 servings

1 large onion, chopped (1 cup)
1 cup chopped celery
3 tablespoons butter or margarine
2 cans (7 ounces each) tuna
1 package (10 ounces) frozen peas
2 cups tomato juice
1 cup water
1 teaspoon salt
1 teaspoon sugar
1 teaspoon leaf basil, crumbled

1 Sauté onion and celery in butter or margarine until soft in a kettle.

2 Drain tuna and break into chunks; stir into onion mixture with frozen peas, tomato juice, water, salt, sugar and basil; cover. Simmer 30 minutes to blend flavors.

3 Ladle into soup bowls; garnish with chopped parsley, if you wish.

Chowder Diamond Head

Chicken, pineapple, and coconut combine for this special chowder

Makes 6 servings

1 cup sliced celery
1 small onion, chopped (¼ cup)
2 tablespoons butter or margarine

½ teaspoon ground ginger
2 cans (10¾ ounces each) condensed cream of chicken soup
1⅓ cups water
1⅓ cups milk
1 can (5 ounces) boned chicken, diced
1 can (about 8 ounces) pineapple chunks, drained
Shredded coconut

1 Sauté celery and onion in butter or margarine until soft in a large heavy saucepan or Dutch oven; add ginger, blending thoroughly.

2 Stir in soup, water and milk Add chicken and pineapple. Heat, stirring frequently, until bubbly-hot.

3 Ladle into soup bowls. Sprinkle with coconut. Serve with hot buttered rolls, if you wish.

Sunday Supper Chowder

End the weekend right with this delicious chowder

Makes 6 servings

1 medium-size onion, chopped (½ cup)
2 stalks celery, sliced
3 tablespoons butter or margarine
2 tablespoons all-purpose flour
½ teaspoon salt
⅛ teaspoon pepper
2 cups turkey broth*
2 large carrots, pared and cut into thin rings
1 package (10 ounces) frozen mixed vegetables
3 cups milk
1 package (8 ounces) process American cheese, diced
1 cup diced cooked turkey
1 tablespoon chopped parsley

1 Sauté onion and celery slowly in butter or margarine in large kettle 5 minutes; remove from heat.

2 Blend in flour, salt and pepper; gradually add turkey broth; heat, stirring constantly, until mixture comes to boiling.

3 Add carrots and frozen mixed vegetables; cover; simmer 30 minutes, or until vegetables are tender; stir in milk, cheese, turkey and parsley.

(continued)

4 Heat slowly, stirring often, until cheese melts and soup is piping-hot. (Do not let soup boil, as it may curdle.)

*TURKEY BROTH

Break up turkey carcass to fit into large saucepan; add 2 cups cold water, 1 sliced onion and a handful of celery tops; cover; simmer 1 hour. Strain broth; if needed, add enough water to make 2 cups.

Macaroni-Cheese Chowder

Quick to make, easy to eat

Makes 6 servings

1 medium-size onion, chopped (½ cup)
½ cup thinly sliced celery
2 tablespoons butter or margarine
2 cans (15 ounces each) macaroni-and-cheese
1 can (about 1 pound) peas and carrots
1 can (14 ounces) evaporated milk
½ cup water
1 teaspoon salt
⅛ teaspoon pepper
½ teaspoon ground marjoram
2 tablespoons chopped parsley

1 Sauté onion and celery in butter or margarine until soft in a large saucepan.
2 Stir in macaroni-and-cheese, peas and carrots and liquid, milk, water, salt, pepper, and marjoram.
3 Heat very slowly, stirring several times, until hot. (Do not boil.)
4 Ladle into a heated tureen or soup bowls; sprinkle with chopped parsley.

Macaroni-Cheese Chowder, hearty enough for a main dish, goes from can to table in about ten minutes.

Brunswick Stew

Chicken, canned soup and vegetables add up to this satisfying meal-in-a-bowl

Makes 8 servings

1 broiler-fryer, weighing about 2½ pounds, quartered
5 teaspoons seasoned salt
Water
1 large onion, chopped (1 cup)
2 tablespoons butter or margarine
2 packages (10 ounces each) frozen Fordhook lima beans
2 cans (11 ounces each) condensed tomato-rice soup
2 cups thinly sliced celery
2 cans (1 pound each) cream-style corn

1 Combine chicken, 3 teaspoons of the salt and 4 cups water in a kettle; cover. Simmer 45 minutes, or until chicken is tender. Take meat from bones; dice. Strain broth into a 4-cup measure; add water, if needed, to make 4 cups.
2 Sauté onion in butter or margarine until soft in same kettle; add lima beans, soup, two soup cans of water and celery; cover. Simmer 15 minutes, or until beans are tender. Stir in chicken, broth, corn and remaining 2 teaspoons seasoned salt.
3 Heat slowly just to boiling. Ladle into heated soup bowls.

Country Chicken Soup

Fast-cook broiler-fryer and cubes of beef go into this made-from-scratch hearty

Makes 8 servings

1½ pounds chuck beefsteak, cut into ½ inch cubes
1 large onion, chopped (1 cup)
1 broiler fryer (2½ to 3 pounds), quartered
1 cup chopped celery
2 teaspoons salt
1 teaspoon seasoned salt
½ teaspoon pepper
½ teaspoon leaf rosemary, crumbled
½ teaspoon leaf thyme, crumbled
1 bay leaf
10 cups water
2 cups uncooked medium noodles

1 Brown beef in its own fat in a kettle or Dutch oven; stir in onion and sauté lightly.
2 Add chicken, celery, salt, seasoned salt, pep-

per, rosemary, thyme, bay leaf and water to
kettle; heat to boiling; cover. Simmer 1 hour,
or until chicken is tender; remove from kettle.
Continue cooking beef 20 minutes, or until
tender; remove bay leaf.

3 While beef finishes cooking, pull skin from
chicken and take meat from bones; cut meat
in cubes. Return to kettle; heat to boiling.

4 Stir in noodles. Cook 10 minutes, or until
noodles are tender.

5 Ladle into soup plates. Sprinkle with chopped
parsley and serve with your favorite crisp
crackers, if you wish.

Chicken Soup with Dumplings

A creamy-thick soup with tender little chicken
balls and vegetables to munch

Makes 6 servings

Chicken Dumplings

1 cup diced cooked chicken
1 cooked chicken liver
1 egg
⅓ cup sifted all-purpose flour
¼ cup milk
1 teaspoon salt
Dash of pepper
Dash of nutmeg
1 tablespoon chopped parsley
1 cup water
6 cups BASIC CHICKEN STOCK (see index for
recipe)

Soup

¼ cup chopped green onion
¼ cup chicken fat, butter or margarine
¼ cup sifted all-purpose flour
1 package (10 ounces) frozen mixed vegetables
½ teaspoon salt
1½ cups diced cooked chicken

1 Combine chicken, liver, egg, flour, milk, salt,
pepper and nutmeg in blender; blend at high
speed until smooth. Turn into small bowl, stir
in parsley; cover.

2 Bring water and 1 cup of the CHICKEN STOCK
to boiling in a large saucepan. Shape chicken
mixture, one-half at a time, into ¾-inch balls
with a teaspoon. Drop one by one into boiling
stock. Simmer gently, uncovered, 8 to 10 minutes; remove with a slotted spoon; keep warm.
Repeat with second half.

3 Saute onion in chicken fat, or butter or margarine in kettle or Dutch oven, until soft but not
brown, 3 to 4 minutes; stir in flour; gradually

add remaining chicken stock, stirring constantly; bring to boiling; add vegetables and salt;
cover. Cook 10 minutes, or until vegetables are
tender.

4 Add chicken dumplings, cooking stock and
chicken; heat 5 minutes. Ladle into soup bowls;
serve with crusty bread.

Mulligatawny Soup

A classic soup, with origins in India, is richly
flavored with exotic curry

Makes 6 servings

3 medium carrots, pared and sliced
2 stalks of celery, sliced
6 cups BASIC CHICKEN STOCK (see index
for recipe)
6 cups BASIC CHICKEN STOCK (see index for
recipe page number)
3 cups cooked diced chicken
1 large onion, chopped (1 cup)
4 tablespoons (½ stick) butter or margarine
1 apple, pared, quartered, cored and chopped
5 teaspoons curry powder
1 teaspoon salt
¼ cup sifted all-purpose flour
1 tablespoon lemon juice
2 cups hot cooked rice
¼ cup chopped parsley
6 lemon slices (optional)

1 Cook carrots and celery in 1 cup stock in a
medium-size saucepan 20 minutes, or until
tender. Add chicken; heat just until hot; cover,
keep warm.

2 Sauté onion until soft in butter or margarine
in Dutch oven; stir in apple, curry powder and
salt; sauté 5 minutes longer, or until apple is
soft; add flour. Gradually stir in remaining
chicken stock; heat to boiling, stirring constantly; reduce heat; cover; simmer 15 minutes.

3 Add vegetables and chicken with the stock
they were cooked in; bring just to boiling. Stir
in lemon juice.

4 Ladle into soup plates or bowls; pass hot
cooked rice and chopped parsley and lemon
slices, if you wish, for each to add his own
garnish. Good with crusty French bread.

Golden Turkey Chowder

When you are in a hurry, this is the soup for you

Makes 4 servings

2 cans (10¾ ounces each) condensed golden
   mushroom soup
2 soup cans of milk
1 can (about 1 pound) cream-style corn
1 cup thinly sliced celery
1 tablespoon instant minced onion
⅛ teaspoon pepper
2 cans (5 ounces each) boned turkey, diced

1 Combine soup, milk, corn, celery, onion and
pepper in a large saucepan. Heat slowly, stirring
several times, to boiling, then simmer 3 minutes
to blend flavors.
2 Stir in turkey. Ladle into a tureen or soup
plates. Garnish with parsley and serve with
bread sticks, if you wish.

Jambalaya Chowder

For a genuine Cajun meal, accompany with
garlic-buttered French bread and chicory coffee

Makes 8 servings

1 medium-size onion, chopped (½ cup)
1 small green pepper, halved, seeded and
   diced
1 clove of garlic, crushed
2 tablespoons butter or margarine
2 cans (10½ ounces each) condensed
   chicken and rice soup
2⅔ cups water
2 large tomatoes, peeled and diced
1 small bay leaf
½ teaspoon chili powder
⅛ teaspoon ground thyme
1 package (about 8 ounces) frozen shelled
   deveined shrimps
1 can (5 ounces) cooked chicken, diced
1 package (6 ounces) cooked nam, cubed

1 Sauté onion, green pepper and garlic in butter or margarine until soft in a large heavy
saucepan or Dutch oven. Stir in soup, water,
tomatoes, bay leaf, chili powder and thyme. (For
easy peeling, place tomatoes in boiling water
for 30 seconds.) Cover; simmer 10 minutes.
Remove bay leaf.
2 Stir in shrimp, chicken and ham; cover. Simmer 10 minutes longer, or until shrimp are
tender. Ladle into soup bowls. Serve with buttered hot biscuits, if you wish.

Copenhagen Oxtail Soup

Savory oxtail soup takes on an elegant look,
garnished with EGGS MIMOSA

Bake at 450° for 45 minutes.
Makes 6 servings

3 pounds oxtails, cut up
3 teaspoons salt
⅛ teaspoon pepper
1 large onion, chopped (1 cup)
2 carrots, pared and sliced (1 cup)
1 parsnip, pared and sliced (¾ cup)
1 turnip, pared and sliced (1 cup)
2 tablespoons brandy
6 cups water
½ teaspoon leaf savory, crumbled
1 bay leaf
   EGGS MIMOSA (recipe follows)
   Chopped parsley

1 Spread oxtails in a single layer in shallow
roasting pan. Roast in very hot oven (450°) 45
minutes, or until nicely browned. Drain off fat,
reserving 2 tablespoons.
2 Sauté onion, carrots, parsnip and turnip in
reserved fat in kettle or Dutch oven, 10 minutes,
or until soft. Add browned oxtails. Drizzle
brandy over, ignite carefully with a lighted
match. Add water to roasting pan in which oxtails were browned. Heat, stirring constantly, to
dissolve browned bits; pour over oxtails and
vegetables in Dutch oven; add savory and bay
leaf. Bring to boiling; reduce heat; cover; simmer slowly 2 hours, or until meat separates
easily from bones.
3 Ladle into soup bowls; place a half egg in
each, sprinkle with parsley. Serve with crusty
French bread.

EGGS MIMOSA
Cut 3 hard-cooked eggs in half lengthwise.
Carefully remove yolks, keeping whites whole.
Press yolks through a sieve, spoon back into
whites.

Some soups take a long time to put together. Not
Golden Turkey Chowder with its canned food basics.
From can opener to the hot soup takes about five
minutes. Serve with a spinach salad for a complete
meal. ⟹

Winter's Best Soup

For a crockery pot version, see index

Makes 6 generous servings

     3 three-inch beef marrow bones
     1 beef knuckle bone, cracked
   10 cups water
     1 can (about 1 pound) tomatoes
     3 medium-size carrots, pared and diced
     2 small white turnips, pared and diced
     1 medium-size onion, chopped
     1 cup diced celery
     6 whole cloves
     1 bay leaf
   ⅛ teaspoon leaf thyme, crumbled
     2 teaspoons salt
     1 teaspoon sugar
   ¼ teaspoon pepper
     1 cup dried lima beans
   ½ pound green beans, diced
     1 cup shell macaroni
     2 cups chopped raw spinach
       MARROW BALLS (recipe follows)

1 Remove marrow from marrow bones to make
BALLS.
2 Combine bones and remaining ingredients,
except lima and green beans, macaroni, spinach and MARROW BALLS, in large kettle.
3 Cover; simmer 1½ hours; add lima beans;
cook 1 hour.
4 Remove bones, skim off fat; add green beans
and macaroni; cover; cook 15 minutes; add
spinach and MARROW BALLS; cover; cook 5 minutes.

Marrow Balls

For a crockery pot version, see index

Makes 24 marble-size balls

   ½ cup mashed beef marrow (from beef marrow
       bones)
     1 cup soft bread crumbs
     1 egg, beaten
     1 tablespoon minced parsley
   ½ teaspoon salt
   ⅛ teaspoon pepper

Combine all ingredients in small bowl; form
lightly into 24 balls.

Penn-Dutch Rivel Chowder

Good but simple cooking was a trademark of
the Pennsylvania Dutch—this one is a good
example

Makes 8 servings

     4 medium-size potatoes, pared and sliced (3
       cups)
     1 large onion, sliced (1 cup)
   3½ cups water
   1¾ teaspoons salt
   ⅛ teaspoon pepper
     1 egg
     1 cup sifted all-purpose flour
     1 can (about 4 ounces) deviled ham
     1 quart milk

1 Combine potatoes, onions, water, 1¼ teaspoons of the salt and pepper in a large heavy
saucepan or Dutch oven; cover. Simmer 15
minutes or until potatoes are tender; remove
from heat.
2 To make rivels (tiny dumplings): Beat egg in
medium-size bowl. Add remaining ½ teaspoon
salt and flour; mix well to form a soft dough;
reserve.
3 Stir ham and milk into potato mixture; heat
just until bubbly; cover. Simmer 2 minutes.
4 Rub a small amount of dough between palms
of hands over kettle of simmering chowder,
allowing tiny pieces of dough to drop into soup,
forming rivels. Simmer about 5 minutes, or until
rivels are tender and soup is thickened.
5 Ladle into soup bowls. Serve with hot muffins,
if you wish.

Old-Fashioned Beef and Vegetable Soup

For a crockery pot version, see index
This hearty soup, chock-full of vegetables and
meat, is a meal in itself

Makes 8 servings

   1½ quarts BASIC BEEF STOCK (see index for
       recipe)
     2 potatoes, peeled and diced (2 cups)
     2 carrots, pared and sliced
     1 cup sliced celery
     2 small onions, peeled and quartered
     1 can (1 pound) whole tomatoes
     2 teaspoons salt
   ⅛ teaspoon pepper
   ½ head green cabbage, shredded (2 cups)
     1 cup frozen corn (from a plastic bag)
     3 cups diced cooked beef
     1 tablespoon chopped parsley

1 Heat BEEF STOCK to boiling in a large saucepan or kettle; add potatoes, carrots, celery, onions, tomatoes, salt and pepper; heat to boiling again; reduce heat; cover; simmer 20 minutes.
2 Stir in cabbage, corn and meat; simmer 10 minutes longer or just until all vegetables are crisply tender. Sprinkle with parsley.
3 Ladle into soup bowls. Serve with chunks of crusty bread.

Beef-Vegetable Potage

Ground meat, macaroni and three vegetables turn into a hearty supper in a hurry

Makes 8 servings

1 pound ground beef
1 tablespoon vegetable oil
1 can (1 pound) diced carrots
1 can (1 pound) cut green beans
1 package (2 envelopes) cream of mushroom soup mix
2 cups diced celery
1 cup uncooked elbow macaroni
4 tablespoons instant minced onion
1 teaspoon salt
2 cups milk

1 Shape ground beef into a large patty; brown in vegetable oil in a heavy kettle 5 minutes on each side, then break up into chunks.
2 Drain liquids from carrots and green beans into an 8-cup measure; add enough water to make 8 cups. Stir into meat mixture, then stir in mushroom soup mix, celery, macaroni, onion and salt. Heat slowly, stirring constantly, to boiling, then cook, stirring often, 10 minutes.
3 Stir in carrots, beans and milk; heat slowly just until hot. Ladle into heated soup bowls.

Borscht

For a crockery pot version, see index
Adding grated fresh beets to soup just before serving gives a beautiful red color. May be served hot or chilled

Makes 6 servings

2 carrots, pared and sliced (1 cup)
1½ cups shredded raw beets
1 turnip, pared and diced (¾ cup)
1 medium-size onion, sliced
1 cup water

2 tablespoons cider vinegar
2 teaspoons salt
1 teaspoon sugar
6 cups BASIC BEEF STOCK (see index for recipe page number)
2 cups diced cooked beef
½ small head of cabbage, shredded (3 cups)
Sour cream

1 In a kettle combine carrots, 1 cup beets, turnip, onion, water, vinegar, salt and sugar.
2 Bring to boiling; reduce heat, cover; simmer 20 minutes. Add BEEF STOCK, beef and cabbage. Simmer 10 to 15 minutes longer or until all vegetables are tender.
3 Stir in remaining ½ cup beets. Ladle into soup bowls. Serve with hearty chunks of homemade bread.

Meat Ball Chowder

For a crockery pot version, see index
Tiny balls of mint-seasoned beef and pork cook in a rich onion broth

Makes 6 servings

¾ pound ground beef
¾ pound ground pork
1 egg
2 teaspoons dried mint leaves, crushed
1½ teaspoons salt
⅛ teaspoon pepper
4 cups water
1 envelope (2 to a package) onion soup mix
1 can (about 1 pound) stewed tomatoes
1 can (about 1 pound) red kidney beans
¼ cup chopped parsley

1 Mix ground beef and pork with egg, mint leaves, salt and pepper in a bowl; shape into tiny balls.
2 Heat water to boiling in a kettle; stir in onion soup mix; cover. Simmer 10 minutes.
3 Place meat balls in simmering soup; cover; simmer 15 minutes. Stir in tomatoes and beans and liquid; heat just to boiling; stir in parsley.
4 Ladle into soup bowls; serve with chowder crackers, if you wish.

Bill Johnston's Manhattan Clam Chowder

A hearty soup developed in Bill's kitchen, on Long Island

Makes 6 servings.

> 36 large chowder clams (quahogs)
> OR: 2 cans (7 to 8 ounces each) minced clams
> ¼ cup (½ stick) sweet butter
> 1 large onion, diced (1 cup)
> 1½ cups diced potatoes (2 medium-size)
> 1 cup diced celery
> ¾ cup diced carrots (2 medium-size)
> ¼ cup diced green pepper
> 1 can (2 pounds, 3 ounces) Italian-style plum tomatoes, drained
> 1½ teaspoons leaf thyme, crumbled
> ¼ teaspoon white pepper
> ⅛ teaspoon curry powder

1 Shuck fresh clams; reserve broth; chop clams coarsely. If using canned clams, drain and reserve broth. Broth from clams should measure 2 cups; if not, add water or bottled clam broth.
2 Melt butter in a large saucepan. Sauté onions until lightly browned.
3 Add remaining ingredients and extra water, if needed, to cover vegetables. Bring to boil; lower heat; cover and simmer 30 minutes, or just until vegetables are tender.
4 Add fresh or canned clams; turn off heat; cover and let stand 2 minutes or just until clams are thoroughly hot. Serve with warm buttered pilot crackers, if you wish.

Looking for a classic chowder to add to your repertoire? Hearty and bold **Bill Johnston's Manhattan Clam Chowder** will fit the bill.

Ham, sausages, macaroni, beans, and vegetables make **Five-Star Soup** one you'll long remember.

Five-Star Soup

The five stars: Ham, sausages, macaroni, beans and vegetables. Big bowlfuls make a hearty main course

Makes 8 servings

> 1 package (1 pound) dried large white navy beans
> 6 cups boiling water
> 1 shank end fully cooked or cook-before-eating ham (about 3 pounds)
> 4 cups shredded cabbage (about 1 pound)
> 2 cups thinly sliced pared carrots (about 7 medium-size)
> 1 large onion, chopped (1 cup)
> 1 cup chopped celery
> 1 clove garlic, minced
> 1 package (12 ounces) smoked sausage links, sliced thin
> 1 can (about 1 pound) tomatoes
> 1 teaspoon salt
> ½ teaspoon pepper
> 1 cup elbow macaroni (half an 8-ounce package)

1 Pick over beans, rinse and place in a large bowl. Pour the boiling water over; cover; let stand 1 hour.
2 Trim several small pieces of fat from ham; melt in a kettle or Dutch oven. Stir in cabbage, carrots, onion, celery and garlic; sauté slowly, stirring often, 20 minutes; remove and set aside for Step 4.
3 Pour beans and liquid into kettle; add ham, sliced sausages, tomatoes, salt, pepper and 6 cups more water. Heat to boiling; cover: simmer 1½ hours.
4 Remove ham from kettle. Cut meat from bone, trim off fat and dice meat. Stir into soup with vegetables from Step 2.
5 Cook 30 minutes, or until beans are tender; stir in macaroni. Continue cooking 15 minutes longer, or until macaroni is tender.
6 Ladle into a tureen or soup bowls; sprinkle with chopped parsley, if you wish.

Note: This soup tastes even better made a day ahead and reheated.

Minestrone

For a crockery pot version, see index
Zesty salami and plenty of vegetables and macaroni go into this Italian favorite

Makes 8 servings

½ pound (1 cup) dried white beans
8 cups water
1 pound salami, skinned and diced
2 cups chopped celery
1 can (about 1 pound) tomatoes
1 cup cubed pared yellow turnip
¼ cup chopped parsley
1 teaspoon leaf basil, crumbled
4 cups shredded cabbage
2 large zucchini, trimmed and sliced
½ cup elbow macaroni
    Grated Parmesan cheese

1 Cover beans with 4 cups of the water in a large saucepan; heat to boiling; cover. Cook 2 minutes; remove from heat; let stand 1 hour.
2 Brown salami with celery in a kettle; stir in beans and liquid, tomatoes, turnip, parsley, basil and remaining 4 cups water; cover.
3 Heat slowly to boiling, then simmer 2 hours. Stir in cabbage and zucchini; simmer 30 minutes longer.
4 Heat soup to boiling; stir in macaroni. Cook 15 minutes longer, or until macaroni is tender.
5 Ladle into soup bowls; sprinkle with cheese.

Minute-Minded Minestrone

A hurry-up soup that's hearty and filling

Makes 6 servings

½ cup finely broken spaghetti
1 cup shredded cabbage
1 cup canned French-style green beans
1 clove of garlic, minced
½ teaspoon salt
3 cups boiling water
1 can (10½ ounces) condensed minestrone soup
1 can (11½ ounces) condensed bean-and-bacon soup
1 can (10½ ounces) condensed vegetable beef soup
    Grated Parmesan cheese

1 Combine spaghetti, cabbage, green beans, garlic, salt and water in a kettle; cover. Simmer, stirring several times, 8 minutes.
2 Stir in soups; heat slowly just until bubbly.

(Soup will be very thick. Add hot water, if needed, to prevent sticking.)
3 Ladle into bowls; sprinkle with cheese.

Scandinavian Supper Pea Soup

This simple yet hearty soup tastes even better made a day ahead and reheated

Makes 8 servings

1 package (1 pound) dried split yellow peas
6 cups boiling water
½ pound lean salt pork
4 cups water
3 large carrots, pared and sliced
1 large leek, trimmed and sliced
1 large onion, chopped (1 cup)
½ teaspoon salt
¼ teaspoon leaf thyme, crumbled
⅛ teaspoon pepper
1 Kielbasa sausage, weighing about 1½ pounds
    Chopped parsley
    Prepared mustard
    Dark pumpernickel

1 Place peas in a heavy kettle; pour in the 6 cups boiling water; cover. Let stand 1 hour. Heat to boiling, then simmer, stirring often, 1½ hours. Press through a sieve or food mill; return to kettle and set aside for Step 3.
2 While peas cook, simmer salt pork in the 4 cups water in a large saucepan 1 hour; add carrots, leek and onion. Cook 1 hour longer, or until pork and vegetables are tender. Remove pork to a cutting board; trim off rind; dice meat.
3 Stir vegetables with broth, pork, salt, thyme and pepper into puréed peas in kettle; lay whole sausage on top. Heat to boiling, then simmer 20 minutes, or until sausage is heated through.
4 Lift out sausage and place on a cutting board or platter.
5 Ladle soup into soup bowls; sprinkle with chopped parsley. Slice sausage to eat with mustard and bread along with the soup.

Even an ordinary luncheon or supper will sparkle with the addition of **Scandinavian Supper Pea Soup.**

Hotdog Hot Pot

A German dish with an American twist

Makes 6 servings

1 pound frankfurters, sliced thin
2 tablespoons butter or margarine
1 large onion, diced (1 cup)
2 medium-size potatoes, pared and diced (2 cups)
2 large carrots, pared and sliced
2 cups water
1 teaspoon salt
1 teaspoon leaf thyme, crumbled
1 tablespoon Worcestershire sauce
1 can (14 ounces) evaporated milk
1 can (12 or 16 ounces) whole-kernel corn
1 tablespoon chopped parsley

1 Brown frankfurters lightly in butter or margarine in a heavy kettle; push to one side. Add onion to kettle; sauté until soft.
2 Stir in potatoes, carrots, water, salt, thyme and Worcestershire sauce. Heat to boiling; cover.
3 Simmer 15 minutes, or until potatoes and carrots are tender. Stir in evaporated milk and corn; heat to boiling.
4 Ladle into a tureen or heated soup bowls; sprinkle with parsley. Serve with chowder crackers, if you wish.

Vienna Sausage Chowder

Reserve this soup for a cold night—and when everyone is hungry

Makes 6 servings

1 medium-size onion, chopped (½ cup)
2 tablespoons butter or margarine
1 can (11½ ounces) condensed split pea soup with ham
1 soup can of water
1 can (10½ ounces) condensed vegetable soup
1 can (1 pound) tomatoes
1 teaspoon marjoram, crumbled
½ teaspoon salt
⅛ teaspoon garlic powder

1 can (4 ounces) Vienna sausages, drained and sliced

1 Sauté onion in butter or margarine until soft in a large saucepan.
2 Stir in pea soup and water; heat, stirring constantly, to boiling. Stir in vegetable soup, tomatoes, marjoram, salt and garlic powder. Heat to boiling again; simmer 10 minutes.
3 Stir in Vienna sausages; heat just until sausages are hot. Ladle into heated soup bowls or plates. Serve with toasted sliced French bread.

Country Pea Soup

One of the oldest recipes, and still a favorite today

Makes about 16 cups

1 package (1 pound) split green peas
8 cups water
4 cups canned tomato juice
1 ham bone or ham hock
1½ cups diced pared potato
1 cup diced celery
1 cup diced onion
1 cup diced pared carrot
1 bay leaf
1 teaspoon salt
¼ teaspoon pepper
1 cup ground cooked ham*
1 egg
2 tablespoons chopped parsley
2 tablespoons all-purpose flour

1 Combine peas, water, tomato juice, ham bone or hock, potato, celery, onion, carrot, bay leaf, salt and pepper in large kettle; bring to boiling; lower heat and simmer, stirring occasionally, 1½ hours, or until peas are mushy-tender.
2 Remove ham bone or hock; cut off any lean meat to grind for ham balls (you will need 1 cup, so buy a meaty hock or use ham left over from a roast); combine ham with egg, parsley and flour; mix well.
3 Form meat mixture lightly into tiny balls (this amount makes about 28); drop into boiling soup about 10 minutes before serving time; simmer to heat through. Serve in big chowder bowls, as this soup is hearty food!

* Meat from bone or hock can be used for all or part of this.

BISQUES AND CREAM SOUPS

Chilled Springtime Soup

So easy and so refreshing! Made in a blender, it's creamy-smooth; in a mixer, tiny bits of the vegetables remain

Makes 8 servings

1 can (10¾ ounces) condensed cream of asparagus soup
1 soup can of water
⅔ cup milk
¼ cup chopped pared cucumber
1 tablespoon finely chopped green onion
½ teaspoon Worcestershire sauce

1 Combine all ingredients in an electric blender or mixer; beat until creamy-smooth; chill several hours.
2 Serve in chilled cups; float thinly sliced cucumber rind on top.

Creamy Spinach Cooler

Popeye might not have approved of this one—but you will

Makes 6 servings

1 package (10 ounces) frozen chopped spinach
2 tablespoons butter or margarine
3 tablespoons all-purpose flour
1 envelope instant chicken broth
  OR: 1 teaspoon granulated chicken bouillon
½ teaspoon salt
⅛ teaspoon pepper
2 cups milk
1 can (14 ounces) evaporated milk
1 small onion, chopped fine (¼ cup)
1 tablespoon lemon juice

1 Unwrap spinach; let stand at room temperature while making sauce.
2 Melt butter or margarine in a medium-size saucepan; stir in flour, chicken broth, salt and pepper; cook, stirring constantly, until bubbly. Stir in milk and evaporated milk; continue cooking and stirring until sauce thickens and boils 1 minute. Remove from heat.
3 Cut partly thawed spinach into ½-inch pieces; stir into hot sauce until completely thawed. Stir in onion and lemon juice. (If you prefer a

smoother mixture, pour soup into an electric-blender container; cover. Beat until smooth.) Pour soup into a large bowl; cover. Chill several hours, or overnight.
4 Ladle into cups or small bowls. Garnish each with a sprig of watercress.

Curried Celery Soup

An unusual, but happy, flavor

Makes 4 servings

½ cup finely diced celery
2 tablespoons butter or margarine
2 tablespoons all-purpose flour
1 teaspoon curry powder
1 teaspoon salt
¼ teaspoon pepper
1 cup skim milk
3 cups water

1 Sauté celery in butter or margarine in medium-size saucepan; remove from heat; blend in flour, curry powder, salt and pepper; gradually stir in milk and water.
2 Cook, stirring constantly, until mixture thickens slightly and begins to boil. Cover; simmer 10 minutes to blend flavors.

Cucumber Cream

Cucumber, chicken broth, and cream blend well for a thick evening soup

Makes 8 servings

3 large cucumbers
3 tablespoons butter or margarine
1 can (13¾ ounces) chicken broth
1 can (10¾ ounces) condensed cream of potato soup
½ teaspoon salt
1 cup light cream or table cream

1 Pare cucumbers; quarter lengthwise; scoop out seeds. Dice cucumbers.
2 Sauté in butter or margarine until soft in a large saucepan. Pour mixture into an electric-blender container; add chicken broth; cover. Beat until smooth; pour back into saucepan.
3 Stir in potato soup, salt and cream. Heat slowly to boiling.
4 Ladle into soup cups or small bowls; float a thin slice of cucumber on each, if you wish.

Guacamole Cream

Become an instant gourmet cook with this guacamole and cream soup

Makes 4 to 6 servings

1 large avocado, peeled and pitted
1 slice onion
1 cup cream for whipping
1 envelope instant chicken broth
½ teaspoon salt
3 drops liquid red pepper seasoning
2 cups milk

1 Slice avocado into an electric-blender container; add onion and ½ cup cream. Cover; beat
until smooth.
2 Beat in remaining ingredients. Chill.
3 Pour into chilled cups or mugs. Sprinkle with
paprika, if you wish.

Mushroom Soup Supreme

Paper-thin slices of fresh mushrooms in rich
bouillon make this dinner starter

Makes 6 servings

½ pound fresh mushrooms
2 tablespoons butter or margarine
2 teaspoons lemon juice
1 tablespoon all-purpose flour
½ teaspoon salt
4 cups water
2 chicken-bouillon cubes
2 egg yolks
1 teaspoon sherry

1 Wash mushrooms; trim ends of stems, then
cut through caps and stems to make thin slices.
2 Sauté, stirring often, in butter or margarine
in a medium-size saucepan 2 minutes. Sprinkle
with lemon juice; toss lightly to mix.
3 Blend in flour and salt; stir in water and bouillon cubes. Heat, stirring constantly until cubes
dissolve, then cook until mixture boils 1 minute.
4 Beat egg yolks well with sherry in a small
bowl; blend in about a half cup of the hot
mushroom mixture, then stir back into remaining mixture in saucepan. Heat, stirring constantly, 1 minute longer.
5 Ladle soup into heated cups or bowls. Serve
plain or with crisp crackers.

Potato-Crab Bisque

This has always been a sea-side favorite—make
it one of yours

Makes 4 servings

1 can (10¾ ounces) cream of potato soup
2 cans milk
1 teaspoon grated onion
⅛ teaspoon curry powder
1 can (about 3¼ ounces) crabmeat, drained,
  boned and flaked
1 teaspoon chopped chives

1 Combine soup, milk, grated onion and curry
powder in medium-size saucepan; heat just to
boiling over medium heat, stirring often; pour
into serving bowl; chill.
2 Just before serving, stir in crabmeat; sprinkle
with chopped chives.

Potato-Cucumber Soup

It's like vichyssoise, with tiny cubes of crisp
cucumber floating in it

Makes 4 servings

1 can (10¼ ounces) frozen condensed cream
  of potato soup
2 cups milk
1 small cucumber, pared and finely diced
  (about 1 cup)
½ teaspoon salt
⅛ teaspoon pepper
2 tablespoons chopped parsley

1 Combine soup and milk in saucepan; heat
to boiling; stirring often.
2 Remove from heat; stir in cucumber, salt and
pepper; pour into medium-size bowl; chill.
3 Serve in cups or small bowls with parsley
sprinkled on top.

Frosty Cucumber Soup

To fix this cool and refreshing summer soup
in a hurry, twirl it in your blender

Makes 6 servings

2 cans (10¾ ounces each) condensed cream
  of celery soup
1 small cucumber, pared and chopped
2 sprigs watercress, chopped
1 tablespoon chopped green onion

2 cups milk
½ cup dairy sour cream

1 Combine soup, cucumber, watercress and green onion in large bowl of electric mixer; beat until mixture turns pale green. (Or if using an electric blender, twirl 1 can of soup at a time and just slice in vegetables. Blender will do the chopping.) Stir in milk; chill until serving time.
2 Spoon into mugs or soup bowls; top each with a spoonful of sour cream; serve with bread sticks, if you like.

Cream of Watercress Soup

A special soup with a refreshing taste

Makes 6 servings

1 bunch watercress
1 tablespoon all-purpose flour
3 cups milk
1 teaspoon instant minced onion
1 teaspoon salt

1 Wash and dry watercress; save 6 sprigs for garnish. Chop remaining stems and leaves (you should have about 1¾ cups).
2 Smooth flour and 1 to 2 tablespoons milk to a paste in medium-size saucepan; slowly stir in remaining milk; add onion and salt. Cook, stirring constantly, until mixture thickens slightly and boils 1 minute.
3 Remove from heat; stir in watercress. Serve at once or keep hot over very low heat. Do not let it boil. (If you prefer the soup puréed, twirl it in an electric blender.) Ladle into heated cups; garnish each with a sprig of watercress.

Country Buttermilk Soup

This tart and refreshing soup will make fans of many who say they don't like buttermilk

Makes 4 servings

2 cups buttermilk
2 cups mixed vegetable juice (from a 46-ounce can)
1 tablespoon sugar
½ teaspoon salt
½ teaspoon instant onion powder
Few sprigs of watercress

1 Combine all ingredients except watercress in medium-size bowl or pitcher; beat to mix well;

chill. (If you have an electric blender, use it to make this soup even faster.)
2 Serve in glasses or cups (it's thin enough to drink); garnish with watercress.

Cream Consommé

A smidgen of curry powder adds a subtle—and delightful—flavor touch

Makes 8 servings

2 small apples
1 medium-size onion, chopped (½ cup)
⅛ teaspoon curry powder
2 tablespoons butter or margarine
2 cans (10½ ounces each) condensed beef consommé
1 cup cream for whipping

1 Pare one of the apples; halve, core, and chop. Sauté with onion and curry powder in butter or margarine until onion is soft in a medium-size saucepan.
2 Spoon into an electric-blender container; add 1 can of the consommé; cover. Beat at high speed several minutes, or until smooth. Pour back into saucepan.
3 Stir in remaining can of consommé and cream. Heat slowly until hot.
4 Ladle into heated soup cups or bowls. Quarter remaining apple; core; slice thin. Float 1 or 2 slices in each cup.
Note: If you do not have a blender, mince the one apple and onion; sauté with curry powder in butter or margarine, then heat with both cans of consommé and cream.

Creamy Tomato-Clam Soup

Serve this chilled so the flavor lingers in your mouth

Makes 4 servings

1 can (10¾ ounces) condensed tomato soup
1 cup buttermilk
1 teaspoon Worcestershire sauce
¼ teaspoon salt
1 can (about 8 ounces) minced clams

1 Beat tomato soup with buttermilk, Worcestershire sauce and salt until smooth in a large bowl. Stir in clams and liquid; cover. Chill several hours or overnight.
2 Ladle into cups or small bowls; garnish each serving with a sprig of parsley, if you wish.

Classic Clam Bisque

One mouthful and you'll realize why this bisque is a classic

Makes 6 servings

1 medium-size onion, chopped (½ cup)
3 tablespoons butter or margarine
3 tablespoons all-purpose flour
2 cans (8 ounces each) minced clams
1 bottle (8 ounces) clam juice
1½ cups light cream or table cream
1 tablespoon tomato paste (from a 6-ounce can)
4 teaspoons lemon juice

1 Sauté onion until soft in butter or margarine in a large saucepan; stir in flour; cook, stirring constantly, just until bubbly.
2 Stir in clams and liquid and clam juice; continue cooking and stirring until mixture thickens and boils 1 minute; cover. Simmer 15 minutes to blend flavors.
3 Blend in cream, tomato paste and lemon juice. Heat slowly just until hot.
4 Ladle into soup cups.

Note: If you prefer bisque smooth, pour mixture from Step 2 into an electric-blender container; cover. Beat until creamy-smooth; return to saucepan and stir in remaining ingredients, following directions in Step 3. To avoid last-minute fussing, soup may be made ahead, chilled, and reheated slowly just before serving.

Quick Clam Bisque

A quick-to-make chilled soup that's hearty yet refreshing. Try it hot in winter, too

Makes 4 servings

1 can (8 ounces) minced clams, drained and rinsed*
2 tablespoons butter or margarine
1 can (10½ ounces) condensed vegetable soup
1 cup light cream or table cream
2 tablespoons chopped parsley
Dash of cayenne

1 Sauté clams lightly in butter or margarine in medium-size saucepan.
2 Remove from heat; blend in soup and cream until smooth; stir in parsley and cayenne; pour into serving bowl; chill.

* We suggest rinsing clams, as the juice may make the soup too salty.

Curried Shrimp Bisque

For this refreshing appetizer, combine canned soup, cream and seasoning—and let your blender do the rest

Makes 6 servings.

2 cans (10¾ ounces each) condensed cream of shrimp soup
2 cups light cream or table cream
½ teaspoon curry powder

1 Combine all ingredients, half at a time, in an electric-blender container; cover; beat until smooth. Chill several hours, or until serving time.
2 Pour into dainty cups or goblets; sprinkle lightly with a few finely cut chives, if you wish.

Frosty Fish Bisque

So rich in flavor—make more than you think is enough because everyone will call for seconds

Makes 8 servings

1 package (1 pound) frozen perch fillets
1 teaspoon seasoned salt
1 bay leaf
2 slices lemon
1 cup water
2 cans (10¾ ounces each) condensed cream of potato soup
2 cups milk
1 cup light cream or table cream

1 Combine frozen fish, seasoned salt, bay leaf, lemon slices and water in a medium-size frying pan. Heat to boiling; cover. Simmer 10 minutes, or until fish flakes easily; remove bay leaf and lemon slices.
2 Break fish into pieces; place fish and cooking liquid in an electric-blender container; cover. Beat until smooth; pour into a large bowl. (If you do not have a blender, flake fish very fine with a fork, then mix with cooking liquid. Soup won't be as smooth but will taste just as good.)
3 While fish cooks, combine potato soup with 1 cup of the milk in a medium-size saucepan; heat, stirring several times, just to boiling. Cool slightly; pour into an electric-blender container;

cover. Beat until smooth. Stir into fish mixture with remaining 1 cup milk and cream; cover. Chill several hours or overnight.

4 Ladle into cups or small bowls; float a thin green-pepper ring and several fish-shape crackers on each serving.

DELICIOUS CHEESE SOUPS

Hale and Hearty Cheese Soup

Here's a soup that makes budget-stretching a delicious pleasure!

Makes 6 servings.

2 tablespoons butter
½ cup chopped celery
2 tablespoons all-purpose flour
3 cups milk
2 cups peeled, cooked, diced potatoes
1 package (10 ounces) frozen peas
1 can (1 pound) salmon, drained, boned and flaked
2 cups shredded Cheddar cheese (8 ounces)

1 Melt butter in a large saucepan; add celery and sauté until tender. Stir in flour; cook over low heat until mixture is smooth. Remove from heat.
2 Stir in milk. Heat slowly, stirring constantly, to boiling; boil 1 minute, continuing to stir.
3 Stir in potatoes, peas and salmon. Heat just until bubbly hot. Add cheese; stir until melted. Garnish with dillweed, if you wish.
Note: For a thinner soup, stir in additional milk, ½ cup at a time, to desired consistency.

Swiss Potato Soup

The mild flavors of cheese and potato blend so pleasingly: and this soup tastes equally delicious hot or cold

Makes 8 servings.

1 large onion, chopped (1 cup)
3 tablespoons butter

3 large potatoes, pared and cut up
1 teaspoon salt
¼ teaspoon dry mustard
⅛ teaspoon white pepper
3 cups water
2 cups milk
8 ounces sliced Swiss cheese, cut up
2 tablespoons chopped parsley

1 Sauté onion in butter until soft in a kettle; stir in potatoes, salt, mustard, pepper and water. Heat to boiling; cover.
2 Simmer 30 minutes, or until potatoes are very soft; press through a fine sieve into a large bowl; return to kettle. Stir in milk; heat slowly just to boiling. Stir in cheese until melted.
3 Ladle into soup bowls or plates; sprinkle with parsley. Or chill several hours and serve cold.

Cheese and Oyster Stew

Serve this as an appetizer or main dish

Makes 4 servings.

¼ cup (½ stick) butter or margarine
2 cups milk
2 cups light cream
½ cup finely grated Romano cheese (2 ounces)
2 tablespoons all-purpose flour
2 cans (8 ounces each) whole oysters, with juice
Salt
Finely chopped chives or green onions
PARMESAN CHEESE TOASTS (recipe follows)

1 Heat butter or margarine with milk and cream in a large saucepan, until butter is melted.
2 Combine cheese and flour in a bowl; stir into saucepan. Stir over low heat just until mixture starts to bubble. Add oysters and juice.
3 Simmer soup 2 minutes. Stir in salt to taste. Pour into individual soup bowls; top with chives. Serve with PARMESAN CHEESE TOASTS.
PARMESAN CHEESE TOASTS
Lightly toast 4 slices of toasting white bread. Then spread evenly with mayonnaise or salad dressing; sprinkle lightly with grated Parmesan cheese. Cut slices in half. Place on cookie sheet and bake in moderate oven (350°) about 5 minutes, or until bubbly hot.

Frank-and-Bean Chowder

Two favorites are made into a special family treat

Makes 6 servings.

1 medium-size onion, chopped (½ cup)
½ pound frankfurters, sliced
2 tablespoons vegetable oil
1 cup sliced celery
1 can (10½ ounces) condensed beef broth
1 can (11½ ounces) condensed bean with bacon soup
1 can (about 1 pound) stewed tomatoes, cut up
1 can (about 1 pound) cut green beans
½ cup shredded Cheddar cheese (2 ounces)

1 Sauté onion and frankfurters in vegetable oil, stirring occasionally, until lightly browned in a large heavy saucepan or Dutch oven.
2 Add celery, beef broth, bean soup and canned vegetables with their liquids; heat just to boiling; reduce heat; cover. Simmer 5 minutes.
3 Ladle into soup plates. Sprinkle cheese over top. Serve with hot refrigerated biscuits, if you wish.

Creamy Florentine Soup

This blender-easy soup is great for warm days, or as a light appetizer course

Makes 8 servings.

2 packages (10 ounces each) fresh spinach
½ cup chopped shallots
3 tablespoons butter or margarine
3 cans (13¾ ounces each) chicken broth
1¼ teaspoons salt
⅛ teaspoon pepper
Dash of ground nutmeg
8 ounces cream cheese, diced

1 Trim spinach; wash leaves well; shake water off.
2 Sauté shallots in butter or margarine until soft in a large skillet. Add spinach; cover. (No need to add any water.) Cook over medium heat 10 minutes, or just until leaves are wilted.
3 Add chicken broth, salt, pepper and nutmeg; simmer 5 minutes; cool slightly.
4 Pour part of the soup, a little at a time, into container of electric blender; cover. Whirl until smooth. (Or purée through sieve or food mill.)

5 Pour into a large saucepan; add cream cheese. Heat gently, stirring constantly, just until cheese has melted into soup.
6 Pour into a bowl. Cover; chill at least 4 hours.
7 Pour into chilled serving bowl. Garnish with sieved hard-cooked egg, if you wish. Serve icy cold.

Brown Swiss Soup

This cousin to French onion soup makes an elegant first course with a minimum of effort

Makes 4 servings.

¼ cup (½ stick) butter or margarine
2 cups frozen chopped onion
2 cans (13¾ ounces each) beef broth
½ cup water
2 envelopes brown gravy mix
4 thick slices French bread
Butter or margarine
1 cup shredded Swiss cheese (4 ounces)

1 Melt ¼ cup butter or margarine in a large saucepan, sauté onion until tender. Add broth and water; bring to boiling. Stir in gravy mix; simmer 5 minutes.
2 Ladle into 4 ovenproof dishes. Spread bread with butter; place one slice in each serving of soup. Divide cheese over the 4 slices of bread.
3 Place dishes in very hot oven (450°). Bake about 3 minutes, or until cheese is bubbly.

INTERNATIONAL SOUP FAVORITES

Soupe au Pistou
(France)

Makes 8 servings

2 quarts boiling water
1 cup dried pea beans
1 bunch of leeks, trimmed, washed, and chopped
2 medium-size potatoes, pared and sliced (2 cups)
1 cup sliced celery

2 medium-size carrots, pared and sliced (1 cup)
3 teaspoons salt
¼ teaspoon pepper
1 package (10 ounces) frozen cut green beans
½ cup broken spaghetti
2 large cloves of garlic, crushed
1 tablespoon leaf basil, crumbled
½ cup grated Parmesan cheese
⅓ cup tomato paste (from a 6-ounce can)
¼ cup olive oil

1 Pour boiling water over dried beans in a kettle or Dutch oven; let stand for 1 hour.
2 Heat to boiling; reduce heat; cover. Simmer 15 minutes. Add leeks, potatoes, celery, carrots, salt, and pepper. Simmer 30 minutes longer, or until vegetables are almost tender; add frozen green beans and spaghetti; simmer 15 minutes longer, or until spaghetti is tender.
3 While the soup cooks, prepare the *pistou* by mixing the garlic and basil in a small bowl; stir in cheese and tomato paste until well blended; add olive oil, a little at a time, stirring constantly, to form a smooth paste.
4 At serving time, thin the *pistou* with ½ cup of the broth from the kettle, then stir into the soup until well blended. Ladle into bowls; serve with additional grated cheese, if you wish.

Pea Potage
(France)

Makes 6 servings

1 package (2 envelopes) green-pea soup mix
Water
2 cans (about 4 ounces each) Vienna sausages, sliced
1 cup shredded carrot
2 tablespoons butter or margarine
2 tablespoons chopped parsley

1 Prepare soup mix with water, following label directions.
2 Sauté sausages and carrot lightly in butter or margarine in a medium-size frying pan; stir into soup along with chopped parsley.
3 Ladle into soup plates. Serve with thin wheat wafers or your favorite crisp crackers, if you wish.

Tarragon Chicken Consommé
(France)

Makes 8 servings

3 cans (10¾ ounces each) chicken broth
2 teaspoons leaf tarragon, crumbled
1 small lemon, sliced
1 small onion, peeled and sliced
4 peppercorns
2 envelopes unflavored gelatin
2 cups (16-ounce carton) dairy sour cream

1 Pour broth into a large saucepan; skim off fat, if any.
2 Stir tarragon, lemon, onion, and peppercorns into broth; sprinkle gelatin over top; let stand several minutes to soften gelatin.
3 Heat slowly to boiling; simmer 5 minutes; strain into a large shallow pan. Cool, then chill at least 2 hours, or until firm.
4 Just before serving, cut gelatin into tiny cubes; spoon cubes, alternately with sour cream, into parfait glasses. Garnish each with a sprig of parsley, if you wish.

Queen's Onion Soup
(France)

Makes 6 to 8 servings

4 large onions, peeled, quartered, and sliced (about 4 cups)
4 tablespoons (½ stick) butter or margarine
1 teaspoon salt
½ teaspoon ground mace
4 cups milk
2 eggs
2 teaspoons parsley flakes

1 Combine onions and butter or margarine in a large saucepan; cook, stirring constantly, 10 minutes, or until onions are golden but not brown.
2 Stir in salt, mace, and milk; heat slowly just to boiling; remove pan from heat.
3 Beat eggs slightly in a small bowl; slowly stir in about 2 cups of the hot onion mixture, then stir back into remaining mixture in pan. Stir in parsley. Ladle into heated soup bowls or cups; serve with saltines, if you wish.

Watercress Frappé
(France)

Makes 8 servings

½ bunch watercress
1 small cucumber
1 can (10¾ ounces) condensed cream of celery soup
1½ cups milk
¼ teaspoon salt
½ cup light cream or table cream

1 Wash and dry watercress, then pull leaves from stems. (There should be about 1 cup.)
2 Pare cucumber; cut into pieces. Combine with watercress leaves, soup, milk, and salt in an electric-blender-container; cover. Beat several minutes, or until smooth.
3 Stir in cream; chill.
4 Pour into small glasses or cups. Float a cucumber slice on each, if you wish.

Egg-Drop Soup
(China)

Makes 6 servings

2 cans (about 14 ounces each) chicken broth
1 egg, slightly beaten
2 tablespoons chopped parsley

1 Heat chicken broth just to boiling in a medium-size saucepan. Pour in beaten egg very slowly, stirring constantly, just until egg cooks and separates into shreds.
2 Ladle into heated soup cups; sprinkle with parsley.

Cucumber Bisque with Caviar Puffs
(Denmark)

Makes 8 servings

4 large cucumbers, pared and sliced
1 tablespoon grated onion
4 tablespoons (½ stick) butter or margarine
¼ teaspoon curry powder
½ teaspoon salt
2 envelopes instant chicken broth
  OR: 2 chicken-bouillon cubes

1 cup water
8 drops liquid red pepper seasoning
1 cup milk
1 cup cream for whipping
  CAVIAR PUFFS (recipe follows)

1 Sauté cucumbers and onion in butter or margarine just until soft in a large saucepan; stir in curry powder, salt, instant chicken broth or bouillon cubes, water, and liquid red pepper seasoning.
2 Heat to boiling, crushing bouillon cubes, if using, with a spoon; simmer 15 minutes, or until cucumber is transparent.
3 Beat mixture, a cupful at a time, until smooth in an electric blender, or press through a fine sieve; return to saucepan. Stir in milk and cream; heat just to boiling.
4 Pour into cream-soup cups; top each with one or two CAVIAR PUFFS.
Note—This soup tastes equally delicious cold. After beating, chill mixture until serving time, then beat again and stir in milk and cream.

Caviar Puffs
(Denmark)

Bake at 400° for 30 minutes.
Makes about 16

¼ cup water
2 tablespoons butter or margarine
¼ cup sifted all-purpose flour
  Dash of salt
1 egg
3 tablespoons dairy sour cream
1 jar (4 ounces) red caviar

1 Heat water and butter or margarine to boiling in a small saucepan. Add flour and salt all at once; stir vigorously with a wooden spoon until batter forms a smooth ball that follows spoon around pan. Remove from heat at once; cool slightly.
2 Beat in egg until mixture is shiny-smooth.
3 Drop by rounded half-teaspoonfuls, 1 inch apart, on an ungreased cookie sheet.
4 Bake in hot oven (400°) 30 minutes, or until puffed and golden. Remove from cookie sheet; cool completely on a wire rack.
5 When ready to fill, cut a thin slice from top of each puff and scoop out any soft centers with a teaspoon. Fill with sour cream; top with red caviar.

INDEX